THE PHONOLOGY
OF ARIZONA YAQUI

with texts

LYNNE S. CRUMRINE

NUMBER 5

ANTHROPOLOGICAL PAPERS

OF THE UNIVERSITY OF ARIZONA

THE UNIVERSITY OF ARIZONA PRESS

Tucson 1961

Copyright © 1961
The Board of Regents of the Universities and
State College of Arizona. All rights reserved.

L. C. Catalog Card Number 61-64124

PREFACE

This analysis is a revision of my master's thesis which was done at The University of Arizona, 1958, under the direction of John Yegerlehner and Edward H. Spicer of the Department of Anthropology. Their advice and aid has been of great value. The research upon which the work was based was made possible through a grant from the Comins Fund, The University of Arizona. I wish to express thanks for the use of tape recorders courtesy of the Department of Anthropology, The University of Arizona, and Mr. and Mrs. Roy Kennedy of Borger, Texas. Both machines are Webcors, Webster-Chicago Model 210.

I am especially grateful for the availability, through the Department of Anthropology at The University of Arizona, of unpublished materials of Jean Johnson and Edward Spicer, and for the careful reading by Muriel T. Painter of this manuscript.

To Refugio Savala I am indebted for the literary interest in the texts, for most of the texts are his spontaneous cultural creations.

Any mistakes in the phonology or the texts are my own responsibility, and not that of any person listed here.

Tucson, Arizona
October, 1961

CONTENTS

0. Introduction 1
1. Eliciting Procedures 2
2. Consonant Phonemes 3
3. Vowel Phonemes 4
4. Stress 5
5. Intonation, Junctures, and Phrasing 6
6. Consonant Clusters 7
7. Vowel Clusters 9
8. Automatic Morphophonemic Alternations 9
9. Non-automatic Morphophonemic Alternations 10
10. Summary 10
    References 11
    Appendix: Yaqui Texts (with interlinear and free translations) 13
        Archives of the Languages of the World Text 13
        Positionals and Directionals Text 27
        Conversation Text 38

TABLES

1. Approximate Values of Consonant Allophones except /w/ and /y/ 3
2. Approximate Values of Vowel Allophones 4
3. Double Consonant Clusters 8

INTRODUCTION

0. Many limitations exist with regard to this study. Not the least of these is the lack of full exploration here of the phonemic systems of the Spanish and English of the informants and the extent of the influence of bilingualism or trilingualism on the Yaqui phonemic systems represented in their speech.

It is a hypothesis well worth investigating that all systems a Yaqui speaker controls exert influences appearing as irregularities in any one system.

One would also expect not only differences in phonemic systems of the speech of monolinguals as compared to that of bi- or trilinguals, but also differences conditioned by generational and geographical differences, none of which are very widely represented by this data. Such are some of the limitations of this paper. The incompleteness or tentativeness of phonemic solutions, such as those regarding tone, should also be emphasized. I have revised my own conclusions on them several times. Gerd Fraenkel (1959) has a very different consonant phoneme inventory in his analysis than is presented here. His paper should be consulted by anyone interested in Yaqui phonemics.

The phonology presented here is that of an Arizona dialect of Yaqui as spoken by Refugio Savala and Fernando Suarez of Pascua, Arizona. Refugio Savala was born in Magdalena, Sonora, in 1903, but came to the United States with his mother at about one year of age. He has lived in Arizona since, attending school in Tucson through the second year of high school. Yaqui was the language of his childhood home. As is not uncommon among Pascuans he speaks Spanish and English also. Fernando Suarez speaks Yaqui and Spanish. The two men are members of the same household.

Recorded sources, other than the tapes made with Refugio Savala and Fernando Suarez, were two tapes of Yaqui words recorded by Edward Spicer in 1953 with a South Tucson informant, Ponciano Flores. I transcribed this material and reelicited the part of it which has been used here from Refugio Savala. Before I collected tapes with an informant I also listened to a recording of an Easter Sermon by Ignacio Alvarez, originally recorded on disc by John Green, Easter, 1941. To facilitate listening, parts of the recording were transferred to tape in the radio and television studio of the Speech Department, University of Arizona. I did no transcription from this recording, though on several occasions I consulted the text edited by Painter, Savala, and Alvarez (1955). For other texts and articles consulted see page 11.

Terms and symbols used in this study are taken from or adapted from the following sources: (1) Use of the symbols [ ] = allophonic transcription; / / = phonemic transcription; and most of the articulatory descriptive terms are from Bloch and Trager (1942: 10–27). (2) The term *macrospan* is used here for a unit analogous to Hockett's (1955: 43–5) unit which he calls *macrosegment*. (3) The term *intonation* and associated concepts, such as *terminal juncture*, are adapted from Pike (1948), Hockett (1955: 45–51), and Trager and Smith (1951: 41–9). Symbols used here are for convenience and clarity. (4) Additional symbols are > for *becomes*, and ~ for *alternates with*. These, along with the numbering system used in this phonology, are in standard use in current editions of *International Journal of American Linguistics*. (5) The principles of phonemics and morphophonemics in general have been drawn from Harris (1951), Bloch and Trager (1948), and Hockett (1958).

ELICITING PROCEDURES

1. Four eliciting techniques were employed in order to get materials to be recorded. The Indiana University Archives of the Languages of the World eliciting drawings were presented to the informant. These evoked long and complex utterances. This entire text is included below.

Next, short English utterances were presented for translation. This method was designed to obtain materials for checking hypotheses regarding tonal contour and juncture phenomena.

The third type of eliciting was directed toward obtaining directional and relational material of use for future morphological study as well as for phonological study. A three-dimensional model of a Yaqui house and yard, with ramada and other typical items, was placed before the informant. Matchstick figures of a man, dog, horse, bird, and housefly were manipulated into different positions with respect to the other elements of the model. An effort was made to cause the stick figures to represent actions that the animals they symbolized would normally perform. The pantomime was done largely without English, except to identify each matchstick figure to the informant. The man walked around the house, lay under the ramada, stood before the house, gathered firewood from the ground and piled it up, picked flowers, and so on. The bird flew in circles above the house, then in one window and out another (or through the house), lit on the ramada, and did other things that birds can do. The housefly walked up and down the wall of the house, and so on. There was some repetition in order to permit the expression of various ways of denoting the same or a similar relationship. The method was successful in stimulating fairly immediate responses of the type intended. The informant entered into the spirit of the play and contrived a cardboard automobile out of a matchcover. (See Positionals and Directionals Text, Part 48.) This entire text is included.

A 17-minute conversation tape was elicited by suggesting to the informants that they talk about their childhood, which they did with enthusiasm. About five minutes of this text is presented here.

Some 60 hours were spent in informant sessions. Of this time, three and one-half hours were spent in recording, resulting in a little over an hour of tape in Yaqui with short English identificatory labels. This forms the bulk of the corpus from which this analysis was made. Eliciting techniques, for sessions other than the conversation, were such that the machine was not recording while the stimulus was presented and the informant contemplated his answers. Thus, the Archives of the Languages of the World text is about 24 minutes long not including the informant's contemplative time. The Positionals and Directionals Text is 15 minutes long, and other Yaqui texts, recorded, though not included here, total about ten minutes in length. None of the timing on these texts includes the informant's contemplative time.

The recorded material was translated by playing back short spans of the tape to the informant and transcribing his slow speech equivalents. Each section of speech was then translated literally according to the informant's segmentation of the text into lexical units. A free translation followed this.

After each translation session the fast speech was transcribed allophonically from the tape and files of slow and fast forms were kept together. Pitch and stress were marked on transcriptions of fast speech.

Filing was begun mainly to discover the status of stress and tone in Yaqui. Lexical items were given separate English equivalents by the informant and were filed on separate slips. Below each item was written the fast speech form. Each occurrence of the item was placed on the same slip and marked according to its position in the running text, and thus on tape. Slips were indexed to Yaqui according to the slow speech forms, and carbons were indexed to English. Files of the word lists transcribed from Spicer's tapes were kept in a separate file.

The space divisions between lexical units in the texts are primarily for ease in reading and remain provisional upon the completion of a morphology of Yaqui.

CONSONANT PHONEMES

2. The consonant phonemes are /p/, /t/, /k/, /f/, /č/, /ʔ/, /b/, /d/, /g/, /m/, /n/, /s/, /h/, /r/, /l/, /w/, /y/ (Table 1).

The phonemes /d/, /f/, and /g/ occur primarily in Spanish loanwords (Spicer 1943; Johnson 1943).

2.1. Voiceless bilabial /p/ has one allophone, an unaspirated bilabial stop [p]. Examples are [ʔápo] *third person singular actor*; [púa] *to pick*.

2.2. Stops /t/ and /k/ are voiceless and unaspirated. They are apico-alveolar and dorso-velar, respectively. /k/ has a backed variant [q] preceding back vowels, and an allophone [k] elsewhere. Examples are [kɛt] *yet*; [qóʔoqó] *hurt*; [buítɛk] *ran*; [tááβu] *cottontail rabbit*.

2.3. Voiceless labiodental /f/ occurs only rarely in this corpus, for example [ánima félihtukan] *Felix, who is now deceased, (personal name)*.

2.4. The affricate /č/ is voiceless and apico-palatal. It has a stop onset and a shibilant release. There is a variant [c] in fast speech in which the release consists of a sibilant. Phonetically the allophones are [tš] ∼ [ts]. Examples are: [čúuβala] *while*; [ʔénči vóʔóβičók] ∼ [ʔénči voʔó βicók] *I watched the road for you (singular)*.

2.5. Glottal stop /ʔ/ is produced by stoppage of the air stream at the glottis. Examples are: [váʔáiya] *white rat*; [ʔɛm mála] *your mother*.

2.6. The labial voiced /b/ has three allophones. These are [b], a bilabial unaspirated stop occurring in initial position, and two fricatives which have a higher frequency of occurrence, bilabial [β] and labiodental [v], occurring in initial and medial positions. Examples are [bóʔó] ∼ [βóʔó] ∼ [vóʔó] *road, path*; [híva] ∼ [híβa] *just, already*.

2.7. Voiced unaspirated alveolar stop /d/ occurs only on two occasions in my corpus, though it occurs in a larger number of instances in other texts consulted. Examples are: [díos] *God*; [dragún] *Dragoon (place name in Arizona)*.

2.8. Voiced dorso-velar stop /g/ has two allophones. Examples are: [góʔi] ∼ [gʷóʔi] *coyote*; [dragún] *Dragoon*.

2.9. Nasal continuants /m/ and /n/ are voiced. The allophone [n] of /n/ is apico-velar, but a dorso-velar allophone [ŋ] occurs preceding /w/, /u/, or /k/. The phoneme /m/ has one bilabial allophone. Examples of nasal continuants are: [síʔíme + íŋ waam + sakáʔalam] *all those who have gone by here*; [mála mééca] *mother moon*;

TABLE 1. *Approximate Values of Consonant Allophones Except /w/ and /y/*

		LABIAL	APICAL	DORSAL	GLOTTAL
STOPS	Unvoiced	p	t	(k, q)	ʔ
	Voiced	(b)	d	(gʷ, g)	
SPIRANTS	Unvoiced	β | f	s		h
	Voiced	(v)			
AFFRICATES	Unvoiced		(č, c)		
NASALS	Voiced	m	(n	ŋ)	
LATERALS	Voiced		l		
FLAPS	Voiced		r		

The following consonant phonemes have been analyzed as having more than one allophone:

/b/ = [b] ∼ [β] ∼ [v]   /c/ = [č] ∼ [c]
/k/ = [k] ∼ [q]   /n/ = [n] ∼ [ŋ]
/g/ = [gʷ] ∼ [g]

The remaining phonemes have relatively narrow allophonic variations: /p/, /t/, /ʔ/, /d/, /f/, /s/, /h/, /m/, /l/, /r/, /w/, and /y/.

[néhpo] *I (actor)*; [ʔáməŋ qóʔom] *down yonder*; [táʔata ʔáməŋ wéčeo] *the sun is falling yonder*; [túʔúriakan] *(it) was good*; [ɪtóŋ usíle] *we were children.*

2.10. Voiceless spirants /s/ and /h/ are apico-alveolar and glottal respectively. Examples are [huu hámút síika + mékka] *the woman went away*. When preceding consonants /h/ is sometimes velarized, and in this position has one mora length: [kúx kúta] *rosary wood*.

2.11. Voiced liquids are apico-alveolar flap /r/ and alveolar lateral /l/. In initial position the flap has a schwa onset. The point of articulation for the lateral, when preceding front vowels, is post-dental. In initial position it may have an aspirated onset. Examples are: [kári] *house*; [ráutya] *rinse out*; [líonóka] *pray*; [wépul] *one*; [ʔápɛla] *third person singular alone*.

2.12. Semiconsonants are voiced /w/ and /y/. The latter is palatal. The former has a dorso-velar variant which occurs in initial position when preceding /o/; a spirant [ɣ]. The allophone [w] occurs in all positions in which the phoneme occurs. In initial position spirantization sometimes occurs, as in [ʰwátən] *wanted*. Examples of /y/ are [yóqo] *tomorrow*; [húya] *brush, bush, tree*.

VOWEL PHONEMES

TABLE 2. *Approximate Values of Vowel Allophones*

		FRONT	CENTRAL	BACK	
		Unrounded	Unrounded	Unrounded	Rounded
HIGH	Higher H.	i	ɨ		u
	Lower H.	ɪ	ɨ	ʊ	u
MID	Higher M.	e	ə	ʌ	o
	Lower M.	ɛ	ə	ɔ	
LOW	Higher L.		a		
	Lower L.		a		

/i/ = [i] ~ [ɪ]   /o/ = [o] ~ [ʌ] ~ [ə]
/e/ = [e] ~ [ɛ]   /u/ = [u] ~ [ʊ] ~ [ɨ]
/a/ = [a] ~ [ə]

3. The vowel phonemes are /i/, /e/, /a/, /o/, /u/. All allophones are voiced, except when in macrospan final, explained below. See Table 2.

3.1. The phoneme /i/ has two variants, high front unrounded [i], and a slightly lower high front [ɪ]. Examples are [bóʔó + túʔúriakən] *the road is good*; [wáh pááriáta nɛ bicə́k] *I saw the farm plain*; [húniʔi] *even (intensive)*.

3.2. The phoneme /e/ has two allophones, the higher mid front unrounded [e] and lower mid front [ɛ]. In fast speech the latter occurs before or after stops /t/ and /k/, as a variant near nasals and in clusters with back vowels. Examples are: [vóó čúkti nɛ yéu síikA] ~ [vóó čúkti ne yéu síikA] *I went out across the road*; [ʔɛmɛʔɛ] *you (plural)*; [kɛt] *yet*.

3.3. The phoneme /a/ has two allophones. These are low central unrounded [a] and mid central unrounded [ə]. The variant [ə] usually occurs adjacent to phonemes /t/, /k/, and nasals, but also occurs elsewhere in fast speech. Examples are [ʔamək] *with or accompanying third person singular*; [čáʔəkə] *after, behind*; [huka wə́h pááriátə nɛ + ʰwáatən] *I remembered (longingly) the farm-field*; [népo náa vičə́k hukə́ ɪsítə] *I myself saw the little child*.

3.4. The phoneme /o/ has three allophones. These are higher mid back rounded [o], slightly lower mid back unrounded [ɔ], and higher mid back unrounded [ʌ]. The allophone [ɔ] varies with [o] following /w/ and /k/, and the /ʌ/ varies with [o] as a first member in clusters with /e/. Examples are: [wɔ́kim] *feet*; [kɔ́ttek] *broken*; [nótte] *return*; [yʌémɛ] *Yaqui (person), Yaqui (language)*; [bwíapo] *on the ground*.

3.5. The phoneme /u/ has three allophones. High back rounded [u] occurs in medial and final positions. Lower high back unrounded [ʊ] occurs in vowel clusters preceding /e/, and varies with [u] near /t/ and /k/. High central unrounded [ɨ] is a variant in slow speech as first member in clusters with mid front vowels and high vowels, as a second member in clusters with the same vowels, and before or after nasals. Examples are: [bʊé?ituk] *because*; [?úsi] *child*; [ᵐbóóta nɛ ʰwáatan ɨnnA] *I wanted the road very much*; [bʊɛkáɛ́kan huɨ vátwɛ] *the river was wide*; [baséranta nɛ áa vičÚ] *I saw the lake*; [vuíβɨɨ́ka] *sings*; [βɨɛkáɛ́kan] *was wide*; see also 3.3.

STRESS

4. Most Yaqui words have stress accent. On this point I am in agreement with Johnson (1943) and Dedrick (1946), that is each stem, compound, or idiom said in isolation is characterized by a relatively stable pattern of relative loudness of syllables, though there is perturbation of this stress in running discourse. For the particular form stress takes in discourse of my informants the texts may be consulted. Stress, as it occurs in the accompanying texts, is marked by an acute accent in order to demonstrate its patterning in discourse relative to other phonemic features.

4.1. It appears that stress and time are significantly related in my informants' speech. In a great majority of the texts stressed syllables are equally timed relative to each other regardless of the number of unstressed syllables between them. That is, within any given pre-composed span it takes about the same time to get from one stressed syllable to the next regardless of whether none or several unstressed syllables intervene. The rhythmical effect is often quite striking, especially when stresses are equally intense (as they are especially so in grammatically parallel structures) and where there is a minimum of accompanying tone variation. For example:

| áu + | lío | nóka | ?ó | ?áu | kúhte?o | ?áu | múhte | + |

to pray, and to cross (oneself) and to bow (to the cross). Note that the monosyllable ?o (probably a Spanish loanword) is stressed or not, according to the placement of stress on key contentives, or content words. (For variations in stress placement see texts.) A new time signature, so to speak, may begin with each juncture. (See 5. for definition of junctures.) This means that stresses, though evenly spaced in time relative to one another, may be absolutely slower in one span than another.

4.2. In vowel clusters each vowel may be stressed, resulting in the following timing pattern:

| (+) hu?u | ?úsi | hámut | ínto | ká——— | —áčin | húni |
| ?á——— | —áne | kía | túa | áman a?a | bít— | —čú # |

hu?u ?úsi hámut ínto kááčin húni ?ááne kía túa áman a?a bítčú # *The girl does not make any gestures but just keeps looking.*

4.3. If words of the span are largely of two or three syllables each, the result may be that every other syllable is stressed.

| népo | náa bi-|-čák hu-|-ká u | sí ta | # |

népo náa (ne-a?a) bičák huká usíta #*I saw the little child.*

INTONATION, JUNCTURES, AND PHRASING

5. In order to facilitate the description of junctures and intonation the construct of macrospan is introduced as consisting of any sequence of phonemes bounded terminally by double cross juncture /#/ or by double bar juncture //, and bounded initially by either of these junctures or silence.

5.1. The defining characteristics of # as used in this analysis are integrated primarily with phenomena of tone and pause, and secondarily with stress and time. Vocoid is defined as any tone-bearing phoneme. Falling tone, which usually starts on macrospan final low pitch level (see 5.5.), always occurs on the final vocoid. Falling tone is succeeded by partially or completely devoiced phoneme(s). This series of phenomena is usually, but need not be, followed by a pause or silence.

5.2. The phonemes /k/, /t/, /m/, /n/, /l/, /s/, /h/, /ʔ/, and all vowels occur in macrospan final in simultaneous occurrence with features which are assignable to # or //.

When preceding # the phonemes /k/ and /t/ are always released, and /m/ and /n/ have semi-voiceless or voiceless variants in this position. If vowel(s) precede final nasals, the vowel(s) may or may not be nasalized, but will be voiced.

Vowel(s) occurring macrospan final, when preceding # juncture, have a marked voiceless off-glide or are completely devoiced. In general, # juncture terminates a macrospan concerned with a statement of fact or (not especially emphatic) opinion. It is used almost exclusively in description and narrative. Examples are: hunu ʔóʔóu tékipánOA # *that man works*; hunu hámut buíbwíka*A* # *that woman sings*; ʔilí čúú tábútat čáʔaka buítékaN # *a little dog is running after a cottontail rabbit*; síhume inín waam + sakáalam*M* # *all those have gone by here*.

5.3. Following are the defining characteristics of //. Rising tone, which is usually preceded by phonemically high tone, always occurs on the final vocoid. Final vowels are voiced. The // juncture occurs terminally, bounding macrospans having three types of general meaning: 1.) rhetorical questions, 2.) polite exclamations and emphatic opinions, 3.) short questions requiring information. In the latter type final vowels are often post-glottalized. Examples of 1.) are: kááhunuén // *wasn't it that way?* ʔémpo ʔáu wáaten // *do you remember?* Examples of 2.) are: héewi húnen áanen // *yes, that's (just) the way he used to be!* héewi // ne ʔáu wáate katíʔín // *(ah) yes! I remember, wasn't it that way (though)!* héewi hunáʔa túa itómak wéweaman // *(oh) yes, that's the one who used to wander about so much with us!* Examples of 3.) are: kééčupéʔ // *is it (the tape recording) not yet finished?* čúʔúʔ // ʔoʔ wóʔí # *(is it) dog or coyote?*

5.4. A plus /+/ juncture has been used to mark a pause internal to the macrospan. The + juncture is preceded by a sustenance of pitch. The same segmental phonemes which occur in macrospan final position also occur preceding + juncture. There may or may not be devoicing of final vocoids. A + juncture phrases a macrospan into smaller units. Examples are: nák ne⁺ ket húni unna ilíčiakan bóetuk ket húni + ne báát únná mékka kóʔomi ku ket húni + káá ʔáman kíbakeka bea ʔemé ne téhwálatune maiyóau + ne⁺ ʔíno uhúʔusáekai # *then, because I was still very young (+), I into the very deep water (+) could not enter; you informed me I had to remain here at the edge (+) nursing myself (#)*; ne ilí + yóʔówe # *I was a little (+) adult*; baséran + buekáekan # *the lake was wide*; ʔáewa ʔinto + ʔáu ómteka + ʔitóm aʔa kónkóntaria itómak yéuʔa síiko # *and his mother (+) used to be angry with him (+) and try to intercept him when he tried to sneak out with us*; ʔitépo náwit + bátwemak lópola ʔáánen # *both of us (+) were alongside the river*.

5.5. There are allophonic pitches other than terminal falling (assigned to #) and terminal rising (assigned to //). These pitches may be called highs and lows, and be represented diagrammatically as follows:

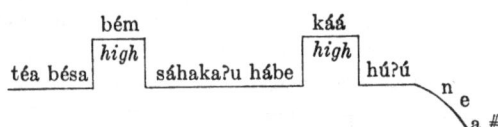

But where they are going nobody knows.

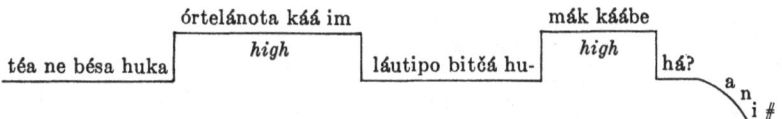

... but I don't see the orchard keeper and he might not be around here.

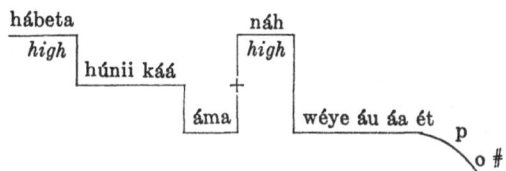

Just anyone doen't walk in his plants.

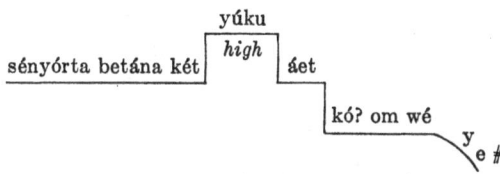

And also from the Lord the rain comes down upon it.

5.6. The choice by a speaker of which segment(s) of a span receive high tones, it may be suggested tentatively, rests upon grammatical and/or stylistic considerations. High and low tones are therefore not written in the texts. In any case, however, tone and stress in running discourse are not to be confused.

5.7. In long narratives, sermons or soliloquies each high tone, though high relative to its immediate environment, is on the same pitch or on an absolutely lower pitch than the last high tone. This goes on from span to span, throughout paragraphs of as many as three or four long macrospans, giving the discourse a descending scale, until the speaker gets a fresh breath. This also is probably a stylistic feature, rather than a phonemic one. This pattern very strongly characterizes the first two texts below, and is quite noticeable in the Yaqui Eastern Sermon (Painter, Savala, and Alvarez, 1955).

CONSONANT CLUSTERS

6. Consonants which occur as second members of consonant clusters are /p/, /t/, /k/, /č/, /b/, /m/, /n/, /s/, /h/, /r/, /l/, /w/, /y/. Consonants occurring as first members of clusters are /l/, /m/, /n/, /k/, /t/, /s/, /h/, /p/, /r/, /b/, and /d/. Those which may occur as third member are /w/ and /y/.

Two clusters of three consonants occur, both with /w/ as a third member: /béngwa/ *long time* (?) and /étbwa/ *steal, sneak.*

Morpheme initial clusters occur in both Spanish and Yaqui words. They seem to be limited, however, to those with /w/, /y/, or /r/ as second member. Examples are: /lwíís/ *Luis (name)*; /kwénta/ *count*; /hwáta/ *tree, (goal)*; /bwána/ *weep*; /pwétata/ *door, gate (goal)*; /nyé/ variant of /ʔínie/ *this*; /dragún/ *Dragoon.*

Most clusters have two members, one of which is on either side of a morpheme boundary. The most common phonemes which occur finally, /k/, /t/, /m/, /n/, /l/, /s/, /h/, and /ʔ/, should, then, be found in combination with all consonants which occur in initial position. This does not seem to happen in a corpus of this size. Those double clusters which were collected are shown in Table 3.

Illustrations of these double clusters are as follows:

/l/ as first member: /wépul púúsim/ *one eye*; /éltúame/ *ease*; /bálko/ *soft, fine, smooth*; /wépul číkul/ *one mouse*; /wépul bóʔóta/ *one road (goal)*; /wépul mééča/ *one moon*; /wépul nóóki/ *one word*; /wépul sontáo/ *one soldier, one chapaiyeka*; /wépul húya/ *a single tree*; /ʔanimálrata/ *animals (all kinds)*; /lúʔulluʔute/ *ending*; /hinélwaači/ *danger*; /wépul yoéme/ *a single person.*

/m/ as first member: /ʔémpo/ *you (singular)*; /sénu yoéme ím táwa/ *one man remained here*; /ʔínim káa yúm hóʔekáʔatek/ *if they did not rest here*; /díos ém čaniábu/ *God help you all, (Hello)*; /ʔámbiča/ *thither*; /báčita itóm mákne/ *it will*

TABLE 3. *Double Consonant Clusters*

First Members of Consonant Clusters

		l	m	n	k	t	s	h	p	r	b	d
S e c o n d M e m b e r s	p	lp	mp	—	kp	tp	sp	hp	pp	—	—	—
	t	lt	mt	nt	kt	tt	st	ht	pt	rt	—	—
	k	lk	mk	nk	kk	tk	sk	hk	—	—	—	—
	č	lč	mč	nč	kč	tč	—	—	pč	—	—	—
	b	lb	mb	nb	kb	tb	sb	hb	—	rb	—	—
	m	lm	mm	nm*	km	tm	—	hm	—	—	—	—
	n	ln	mn	nn	kn	tn	sn	hn	pn	—	—	—
	s	ls	ms	ns	ks	ts	ss	hs	ps	rs	—	—
	h	lh	mh	nh	kh	th	—	hh	ph	—	—	—
	r	lr	—	—	kr	—	—	—	—	—	—	dr
	l	ll	ml	nl	kl	tl	—	—	—	—	bl	—
	w	lw	mw*	nw	kw	tw	sw	hw	pw	—	bw	—
	y	ly	my	ny	ky	ty	sy	hy	py	—	—	—

* These forms occur in slow speech only.

give us corn; /háhámne/ *will reach, overtake*; /símsuk/ *(singular actor) has gone*; /yúm hoéria/ *resting place*; /símla/ *gone*; /ʔím wáin/ *hither (slow form only)*; /ʔiním yúm hóebáe hu ʔúsi/ *the boy wants to rest here*.

/n/ as first member: /ʔíntok/ *also, more, moreover*; /ʔaʔa nánkine ʔau nóitine/ *to go and see (third person singular) and return*; /ʔénči/ *you (singular)*; /kópánbáe/ *wants to rest*; /ʔín mámpo/ *in my hand (slow speech only)*; /ʔúnná/ *very, too, much*; /ʔamánsu/ *up yonder*; /ʔápo hunén hiúne/ *thus he will say*; /ʔíʔan láutipo/ *now presently, immediately*; /ʔamán wameʔe/ *those yonder*; /ʔínye/ *this (fast form)*.

/k/ as first member: /wókpo/ *on foot*; /ʔáu rúkte/ *approach it*; /hékká/ *shelter, shade, ramada*; /káá túik bítčakáʔatek čeá húni/ *not good if (she) see bad trouble*; /ʔinépo aʔa núk búitek/ *I ran away with it*; /humak mééča láuti yéu wéene/ *maybe the moon will come out early*; /mákne/ *will give*; /háksa/ *where*; /yúkumak huʔu báso yuʔín tobóktila/ *the grass has risen with the rain*; /bwíkriʔáane/ *would be singing*; /bóómak lópolá ne síika/ *I went along beside the road*; /né humak émak wéʔetek/ *maybe if I go with you (singular)*; /huáta betúk yúm hóʔene/ *rest underneath the brush*.

/t/ as first member: /ʔétpo/ *among the plants*; /nóttibáe/ *want to return*; /yúku áet kóʔon wéye/ *rain falls on it*; /ʔámet čáaʔaka/ *after them, behind them*; /wíkit bóa/ *bird's feather*; /ket méeča beméla/ *the moon is still new*; /kátne/ *will walk*; /ʔátsúk/ *laughed*; /ket humak/ *yet maybe*; /bítla/ *have seen*; /wíkit wókim/ *bird's feet*; /hámút yóʔówe/ *elder woman*.

/s/ as first member: /wáspo wáhíwa/ *within the farmfield*; /nábústia/ *beyond, through*; /pásko/ *fiesta*; /ʔósbóta/ *blood*; /limósna/ *contribution*; /tébóh bás siáliku búibwíte/ *the little gopher runs on the grass*; /ʔám teswáne/ *inform them*; /ʔúsyóli/ *beautiful*.

/h/ as first member: /néhpo/ *I*; /nábúhtia/ *beyond, through*; /kúh kúta/ *rosary wood*; /ʔóhbóta/ *blood*; /wáhmak/ *(beside the) farmqeld*; /limóhna/ *contribution*; /tébóh báh siálikú búibwíte/ *the little gopher runs on the grass*; /púhhubaka/ *facing*; /ʔám tehwáne/ *inform them*; /ʔúhyóli/ *beautiful*.

/p/ as first member: /píppim/ *breasts*; /kópta/ *forget*; /hápči/ *father, sir, (woman speaking)*; /núnupne/ *will carry*; /hiápsi/ *heart*; /mámap híba/ *just by hand*; /pwéblo/ *town*; /kapyeo/ *sheep herder*.

/r/ as first member: /nórte/ *north*; /súrbétana/ *from or toward the south*; /ʔabérsi/ *if to see*.

/b/ as first member: /pwéblo/ *town, people in a*

ceremony; /yoéme hí?íbwan/ *the man was eating*.
/d/ as first member: /dragún/ *Dragoon (place name)*.

The Spanish loanwords or names which occur in the corpus have been included in these statements, but they by no means exhaust all the clusters from Spanish used by Yaquis. An example is /g/ and /r/ in /milagrosom/ *miraculous* (Painter, *et al.*, 1955: 42, line 104). Many others could be cited which do not appear in these texts. Though large numbers of these consonant clusters are quite possible in Yaqui discourse the very rarity of their appearance might be said to indicate that the Yaqui consonant cluster restrictions operate against the selection of Spanish words with difficult clusters in the speech of my informants.

VOWEL CLUSTERS

7. All combinations of two vowels occur. (See 8.1.) Examples are: /níím/ *here (fast form)*; /?ínie/ *this*; /benásia/ *like, as if*; /hiókwe/ *pardon, forgive*; /hiúbae/ *want to say*; /hú?unéiya/ *know*; /weéya/ *go*; /?ála?éa/ *well (in good health)*; /wéčeo/ *falling*; /teúne/ *will find*; /háisa/ *how*; /kópánbáe/ *want to rest*; /?a?a máaka/ *give it*; /hiáo/ *saying*; /?áunóoka/ *talk to (third person singular)*; /wói/ *two*; /?amayóe/ *escape*; /hóara/ *house, home*; /nóókim/ *words*; /?ó?óu/ *man*; /tuísi/ *very*; /búé?ituk/ *because (slow form)*; /buána/ *weep*; /sénu ?ó?óu/ *a single man*; /púúsim/ *eyes*.

7.1. Usually vowels in clusters are carefully articulated. Occasionally, however, /i/ becomes /y/ following /n/, as in /?ínie/ > /?ínye/ *this*. In addition /u/ > /w/ following either medial allophone of /b/, as in /búía/ > /bwía/ *ground, earth*.

7.2. A few clusters of three vowels were recorded in fast speech, but all have variants in slow speech in which the clusters are eliminated or limited to two members through insertions of glottal stop of /h/, /y/, /w/. Examples are: /hiáo/ > /hiá?o/ *saying*; /kóokósi áuk/ > /kó?okósi ?áyuk/ *is hurt*; /búíapo/ > /bwíapo/ *on the ground*.

AUTOMATIC MORPHOPHONEMIC ALTERNATIONS

8. Morphophonemic alternations which are determined only by phonological environments (in addition to those listed in 7.1.) are listed in the following subsections.

8.1. /h/ and /?/, when intervocalic, may drop out while the vowels may fuse, or if identical, form geminate vowels. This is common in long macrospans. The same statement applies to /y/. Examples are: /húya/ > /húa/ *tree*; /bó?ó/ > /bóó/ *road, path*; /?áiyakáme/ > /?ákame/ *rattlesnake*; /kéhé/ > /kéé/ *not yet*.

8.2. /h/ alternates with /s/ as a first member in consonant clusters, and seems to be the preferred variant. For examples see 6.

8.3. /m/ alternates with /n/ in fast speech, when preceding /w/ and /k/. Examples are: /?im/ *here* + /wa?am/ *by* > /?ínwaam/; /?ínto/ *and* + /?itóm/ *us* + /gómgómtane/ *will (used to) scare us* > /?íntitón gómgómtane/.

8.4. In fast speech /n/ > /m/ preceding /m/ and /p/, as in /baséran/ *lake* + /-ta/ > /baséranta/ *lake (goal)*, but /baséran/ + /-po/ > /baserámpo/ *on the lake*; /?ín-/ *my* + /mámpo/ *in hand, on hand* > /?immámpo/ *in my hand (fast speech)*.

8.5. In macrospan initial, a /?/ plus vowel sequence or /h/ plus vowel may drop out in fast speech. This may or may not be accompanied by compensatory lengthening of an identical vowel in the succeeding syllable. Examples are: /?íním/ > /níím/ *here*; /húnu/ > /nu/ *that*; /huká?a/ > /ka/ *that*.

8.6. In fast speech /f/ alternates with /p/, as in /ápo/ ~ /áfo/ *third person singular actor*.

NON-AUTOMATIC MORPHOPHONEMIC ALTERNATIONS

9. There are many morphophonemic alternations determined by morphological environments. In order to be anywhere nearly thorough in listing these alternations a dictionary would be required. Some examples of different types are as follows: /káata/ apparently alternates freely with /kárita/ *house (goal)*; /bué ʔituk/ > /bóetuk/ *because*, in fast speech; /téa/ > /tá/ *but, on the other hand*. In some words /g/ > /w/, as in /góʔi/ > /wóʔi/ *coyote*. A number of slow speech forms which have patterned changes in fast speech are as follows: /háksa/ *where* + /humeʔe/ *those* > /háksumeʔe/; /hákun/ *where* + /húniʔi/ *even* > /hákuniʔi/; /ʔíʔan/ *now* + /ʔínto/ *and* + /húči/ *again* > /ʔíʔantúči/; /ʔínto/ *and* + /hitása/ *what* > /ʔíntása/; /ʔínto/ *and* + /ʔáu/ *to or of third person singular* > /ʔíntau/; /ʔínto/ *and* + /ʔíʔan/ *now* > /ʔíntiʔan/; /ʔínto/ *and* + /ʔíním/ *here* > /ʔíntim/; /ʔínto/ *and* + /ʔiʔi/ *this* > /ʔíntiʔi/; /ʔínto/ *and* + /húči/ *again* > /ʔíntuči/; /ʔínto/ *and* + /húka/ *that (goal)* > /ʔíntuka/; /ʔínto/ *and*; /húʔu/ *that* > /ʔíntuu/; /káá/ *no, not* + /hábe/ *someone* > /káábe/ *no one*; /káá/ *no, not* + /híta/ *something, thing* > /káíta/ ~ /kahíta/ *nothing*.

SUMMARY

10. This analysis has resulted in a five-vowel system and a relatively small consonant inventory which are closely similar, with minor variations, to the system of writing Yaqui which has become traditional in anthropological literature, as well as among Yaquis.

Some additional conclusions include the following: Stress in single words may be governed by a fuller context in the phrase or sentence where stress and time are significantly related. Grammatical and semantic considerations seem to constitute the governing elements in the use of tone. There are three types of junctures, whose main phonological correlates are tone and pause. Clustering of consonants in Yaqui is quite limited, with some restriction on clusters of two consonants and a severe restriction on consonant clusters of more than two members, even in loanwords. Clusters of two vowels, however, are common and combinations are exhaustive of possibilities. A few triple clusters of vowels occur, though rarely. Vowel clusters are often created through the dropping out of certain consonants in fast speech.

The texts constitute utterances freely and entirely composed by the informants in response to visual stimuli or in the course of Yaqui conversational give-and-take.

REFERENCES

Barber, Carroll G.
   1952 Trilingualism in Pascua, The Social Functions of a Language in an Arizona Yaqui Community. MS, master's thesis, University of Arizona, Tucson.

Block, Bernard, and George L. Trager
   1942 *Outline of Linguistic Analysis*. Linguistic Society of America, Baltimore.

Buelna, Eustaquio
   1891 *Arte de la Lengua Cahita, por un Padre de la Compañia de Jesus*. Imprenta del Gobierno Federal, Mexico.

Dedrick, John M.
   1946 How Jobeʔeso Roʔi Got His Name. *Tlalocan*, Vol. 2, No. 16, pp. 163–66. Mexico.

Fraenkel, Gerd
   1959 Yaqui Phonemics. *Anthropological Linguistics*, Vol. 1, No. 5, pp. 7–18. Bloomington.

Giddings, Ruth W.
   1945 Folk Literature of the Yaqui Indians. MS, master's thesis, University of Arizona, Tucson.
   1959 Yaqui Myths and Legends. *Anthropological Papers of the University of Arizona*, No. 2. Tucson.

Hale, Kenneth
   1959 Internal Diversity in Uto-Aztecan: II. *International Journal of American Linguistics*, Vol. 25, No. 2, pp. 114–21. Baltimore.

Harris, Zelling S.
   1951 *Methods in Structural Linguistics*. University of Chicago Press, Chicago.

Hayes, Alfred S.
   1954 Field Procedures While Working with Diegueño. *International Journal of American Linguistics*, Vol. 20, No. 3, pp. 185–94. Baltimore.

Hockett, Charles F.
   1955 A Manual of Phonology. *Memoir of the International Journal of American Linguistics*, No. 11. Baltimore.
   1958 *A Course in Modern Linguistics*. Macmillan, New York.

Johnson, Jean B.
   1943 A Clear Case of Linguistic Acculturation. *American Anthropologist*, Vol. 45, No. 3, pp. 427–34. Menasha.

Kurath, William, and Edward H. Spicer
   1947 A Brief Introduction to Yaqui, A Native Language of Sonora. *University of Arizona Bulletin*, Vol. 18, No. 1, *Social Science Bulletin*, No. 15. Tucson.

Painter, Muriel T., Refugio Savala, and Ignacio Alvarez (editors)
   1955 A Yaqui Easter Sermon. *University of Arizona Bulletin*, Vol. 26, No. 6, *Social Science Bulletin*, No. 26. Tucson.

Pike, Kenneth L.
   1947 *Phonemics: A Technique for Reducing Languages to Writing*. University of Michigan Press, Ann Arbor.
   1948 *Tone Languages: A Technique for Determining the Number and Type of Pitch Contrasts in a Language, with Studies in Tonemic Substitution and Fusion*. University of Michigan Press, Ann Arbor.

Scoggins, Lois Lynne
   1958 Phonology of Arizona Yaqui. MS, master's thesis, University of Arizona, Tucson.

Spicer, Edward H.
   1943 Linguistic Aspects of Yaqui Acculturation. *American Anthropologist*, Vol. 45, No. 3, pp. 410–26. Menasha.

Taub, Amos
   1950 Traditional Poetry of the Yaqui Indians. MS, master's thesis, University of Arizona, Tucson.

Trager, George L. and Henry Lee Smith, Jr.
   1951 An Outline of English Structure. *Studies in Linguistics: Occasional Papers*, No. 3. Norman.

APPENDIX

TEXTS

The symbols used on the following texts are explained in the phonology, with the exception of the Arabic numerals, which have no significance in Yaqui. They are used only as a convenience in marking segments for the free English translation. Word and phrase divisions are to some extent arbitrary except where marked by double bar (//), double cross (#), or plus (+) junctures, which are phonological divisions natural to Yaqui.

With respect to the English meanings given in these literal and free translations I would like to add a word of caution. It is generally impossible to carry in a single English word the full implications of a Yaqui word, or *vice versa*. For example Mrs. Painter has pointed out that the translation here of *muhte* (Positionals and Directionals Text, Section 5, Number 3.) as "genuflection" is perhaps inadequate, since the word implies "the whole act of veneration," not just genuflection; the translation of *lionooka* (Positionals and Directionals Text, Section 10, Number 1.) as "blessing" might perhaps better be translated in all its contexts as "pray," and so on. It is hoped that a Yaqui grammar and a dictionary exploring such meaning subtleties will someday be made generally available.

ARCHIVES OF THE LANGUAGES OF THE WORLD TEXT

1

1. ním hámanak bóó bóʔoka + 2. níika + huyáta báhi tátakalaim awakáʔapo ne wáʔám siika
   here where-some road lies   of-this   tree   three forks   points-at I by   went
ne ʔáu wáate   # 3. hunáe bóʔówi # 4. ʔíntok + níi húya hunúk + káá ínien síaliakan ían
I to-it remember   that road-on   and   this tree then   not like-this green-was now
íntok uhúyoisi + sáwák   #
and beautifully leaves-with

1. There's a road going through here somewhere. 2. This tree with the three forks, I remember when I went by it 3. on this road. 4. This tree was not so green and now it's beautiful with leaves.

2

1. katíín ne éu   nóókan + waʔa yoéme iním waʔam + bóʔóta bóʔoka + tían iníka huáta
   not-did I to-you talk   that man   this by   road   lies   says this tree
wéekaʔapo ámani # 2. háibu ápo iniét + huám símela   máčéa + 3. húʔunakiačim + aʔa
stands-where by   already he on-this trees went-through so-that visible   him
wók sukáʔapo   ámani #
foot where-he-has-stepped by

1. Did I not tell you that man says there lies a road through here where this tree stands? 2. He has gone through here. 3. His footprints are visible.

13

3

1. iníka yoémta sehtúl in wa'am síkame yoéme sí'ime + 'ían + iníka wepúl bó'óta i'an
   this man once here by went man all now this one road now
iniét + yá'alamtákai # 2. wówóika babáhika náu réhta waté into huyáta betúkun +
this-way made have two three together walk some and tree under
kopánbáekái amán rúkte #
shelter-desiring-to-take there approach

1. As this man went by here everyone of these men have started using this road. 2. Two and three are walking together. Some approach under the tree to take shelter, desiring to take shelter under it.

4

1. tiémpota yumák + 2. imé yoéme + ket húnika huyáta haháse né intók # 3. káá yúm
   time came these men yet even-this tree follow I and not tiredness
hóeriata? + íno háriúriaka kiá ket húni nábuhti wéye? # 4. wame yoéme inín wá'am
resting myself looking-for already yet still beyond going those men here by
sáhakáme # 5. ín hahámbáe bé̌či'ibo #
traveled I reach-want because

1. As the time came, 2. the people are looking for shelter, but 3. I myself do not seek any shelter 4. but I will continue going ahead, 5. because I want to overtake the other men who have gone through here.

5

1. hó'o wúsim emé híba hú'únea + 2. (yu) + yúm hó'oebáetek húni + 3. iní wepúl
   see boys you(plu) already know tiredness to-rest-want even this one
huyá hiba (iním) + i'anía bó'óta áyúk + 4. í'an láutipo # 5. á'a únná tatáa humák húni ite
tree just on-this road exists now presently it's very hot perhaps still we
nábuhti sáhákateka waam séka'ana yúm ho'ériata hahámne #
beyond travel-if there the-other tiredness rest reach-will

1. See boys, you know, 2. if you want to take a rest, 3. only this tree is on this road. 4. Now, for the time being, 5. it's very hot. Perhaps if we go beyond, we will reach the rest at the next place.

6

1. két né hunén hiáusuhú # 2. sénu yoéme i'im táawabáe húmakú'u # 3. 'ité húma wóika
   yet I thus saying and one man here remain-wants probably we may two-being
káá báeka húni'i nábuhtia kátne # hum séká'ana itóm + yahá'apo táhtia + 4. hunáman te
not wanting even beyond go-will there the-other we arrive-at until down-yonder we
hú'úbwa + yúm hó'ene #
a while tiredness rest-will

1. And now, as I was saying, 2. one man probably wants to remain here. 3. Maybe we, there being two of us, even if we don't want to, will have to travel until we arrive at the other place. 4. Then we will take a rest for a while.

7

1. níika huáta ne + háiwaka wéye 2. í'an ála né hekkáta betúk yúm hóene # 3. yoémen ín
   this-is tree I seek-ing go now then I shade under tiredness rest-will men horo

waʔam sáhakámené # wók hahásé?etek 4. húmak # yóko háksa táʔata wéʔepo húmak ne
   by   went-who-I   tracks follow-if   maybe tomorrow somewhere sun   going maybe I
ʔám hahámne #
them overtake-will

1. This is the tree I am looking for. 2. Now I will rest under the shade. 3. If I follow the tracks of the men who went through here, 4. maybe tomorrow sometime (*lit.* the sun going somewhere) maybe I will overtake them.

8

1. iním huáta betúk yúm hóʔelá # 2. humak húu ʔúsi hámút amet čáʔaka wéeme ket
    here tree beneath tiredness rest-have   maybe the child female them after walk-who also
humak nábusti símsuk # 3. ité íntok + káá im yúm hóeka # 4. ʔámet čáʔaka kátné +
maybe beyond gone-has   we and   not here tiredness rest-ing   them after go-will
5. humák ité + yúm hóekáʔatek 6. ʔám sakáʔasuk # 7. káʔam háámne #
   maybe we tiredness rest-if   them gone   not-them overtake-will

1. They have rested here under the tree. 2. Maybe the girl who was following them has gone on beyond here. 3. We shouldn't rest here. 4. We should continue going after them. 5. Because perhaps if we rest, 6. they will be gone, 7. and we will not overtake them.

9

1. ʔínto te waam sénu yúm hóería ám háámne + 2. bóetuk wáme + ʔínim káa yúm
   and we there one resting place them overtake-will   because those   here   not tiredness
hóekáʔatek 3. waam sékáʔana yúm hóʔeria (híba yu) híba yuʔín čúúba ááne #
rested-if   there the-other resting place   always much while stay-will

1. We shall overtake them over there at the other resting place, 2. because if they did not rest here, 3. they will probably stay for a while at the next resting place.

10

1. ʔiním yúm hóebáetek ʔémpo + (ʔím) + ʔim tawáne 2. ʔinéhpo húči nóttibáe #
   here tiredness rest-want-if you(s.)   here stay-will   I   again return-want
3. ʔémpo ínto nábuhti sikáa amán waameʔe batóʔim + 4. ʔam háhámekáʔatek # húči nótteka
   you(s). further beyond going yonder those   people   them overtake-if   again returning
ínwáin hóʔarau né téhwáne #
hither home-to me tell-will

1. If you want to rest here you can remain. 2. I am going to return, 3. and you go on through yonder to those people. (*lit.* baptised ones) 4. If you overtake them return here to my home, and tell me.

11

1. ʔiním yúm hóebáe húu ʔúsi + 2. ʔitépoté + nábuhti sáhaka amán wamé # 3. wame
   here tiredness rest-wants the boy   we-shall   beyond going yonder those   those
ínwaʔam sahakáme (haháne) ʔámahúni te ham + hahámekáʔatek # yókó + ʔámeu
here-by went-who   maybe we them   overtake-them-if   tomorrow to-them
yáhiné #
arrive-will

1. The boy is going to rest here. 2. We shall go on beyond to those who have (already) gone by here. 3. Perhaps if we overtake them we shall reach wherever they are tomorrow.

12

1. huka?a úsita ím + huyáta betúk + yúm hó?báe?o # 2. ?inépo ne hóeráu bičá húči
   this boy here tree under tiredness rest-wants-if myself I home-to toward again
nóttine # 3. ?emé ?íntok hum + nábuhti wame bató?im + wókit saháka # 4. ?am háámeka +
return-will you(pl.) and there beyond those people tracks going them reach
tó?étek húnii + ámmak étehótek hunii húči nóttek íntuči íim hóarau # (ne)
lay-down-to-sleep-if even them-with talk-if even again returning and-again here home
néwa?a + lutúria mákne? #
to-me truth give-will

1. If the boy wants to rest here under the tree, 2. I am going back home again. 3. And you, going beyond, follow the footprints of the people who went by. 4. If you should reach them before night, if you talk to them, then return again to my home and tell me about them.

13

1. (?inépo) népo káa yóotáka iním + nukísi hiba + hú?utéata hipúe # 2. wame bató?im sí?íme +
   myself not grown-being here as-far just strength have those people all
nábúhti + sáhakáme # ne káa háibu ?am hahámne 3. íntok húmak + ne káa ?ám téakáatek #
beyond went-who I not never them reach-will and maybe I not them find-if
?ínepo íntok íno tá?aruká?atek 4. čéa húni káá tu?íne #
I and me lost-if worse even no good-would-be

1. Myself not being grownup, this is as far as I have strength to go. 2. As for those people who have gone through here, I will never reach them. 3. And perhaps if I don't find them, I will get lost, 4. and that would be awful. (*lit.* that would be even worse than not good.)

14

1. sí?íme + inín wa?am saká?ala + hó?oben hume + bató?im tá ne + 2. népo káá amán
   all here by went it's-true those people but I myself not yonder
yumáka 3. iním tá?áwak # 4. ?áhta ne énči yepsá?u tahtia im énči bó?obitčák 5. ?i?án
reaching here remained until I you(s.) arrive until here you(s.) road-watched now
su íntok + ?émpo # káá ?im yúm hó?ebáetek húni?i + 6. né humak émak wé?etek húmak
and more you not here tiredness rest-want-if even I maybe you-with go-if maybe
túi?isi wéene 7. tá inépoláne káa ?áman íno páppéya #
right go-will but I-alone not yonder myself feel-like

1. It's true that all the people have gone by here, 2. but I could not make it there, 3. so I remained here.
4. I waited for you until you returned. 5. And now if you don't want to rest here even, 6. I may go with you. Maybe I will be all right going with you, 7. but I don't feel strong enough to go alone.

15

1. sí?íme hume + (im) ?ín waam saká?álam + hábe húni (kéé) + kée biná bičá nottíla
   all those here by gone-have none even not-yet hither toward returned
2. bóetuk hu?u + wóki káá (am) + ámbiča sí?íme bó?o hóalá?me # 3. hume?e bató?im sáhakáme +
because the track not thither all road made-who those people went-who
kéé hábe nóttek + 4. í?an íntok éme?e # ámbičá katéme ket + hunáman séká?ana huyáta
not none return now and you(pl.) thither to-who yet even-there the-other tree
wé?eká?u# ?ámeu yaháka?atek + ?ámeu yáhine 5. bóetuk náalemóot kopának wáate (nat) +

stands   them-to reach-if   them-to reach-will   because separately shelter want
nátepola katéme # 6. ʔémo tóʔo saháka nábuhti bóʔota bwísaka huntuan   hume yáhisakame amá
they   go-who   they leave going yonder road   taking   that's-why those arrive-who there
kopánaka bea   # 7. ʔáma + háhámekaʔatek hume mečúkula katéme háhámne #
resting   already   there   reached-if   those last   go-who reach-will

1. Of all those who have gone by here none have returned yet. 2. because their tracks show they have only traveled the other way. 3. Those people who have gone through here, none of them have returned; 4. and now you who are going the same way, if you reach them, you will reach them where the other tree stands; 5. because they are resting separately, they are traveling in separate groups. 6. They go and leave, taking the road beyond. So those who arrive rest there, 7. and if you reach them you will reach those who were last.

16

1. ʔiní ilí   ʔúsi túa né áet + ʔeʔáosu + ʔím + táwaka   kopánbáe humák ne 2. káá
   this little child truly me upon   depending   here   remaining rest-wants maybe I   not
báeka   húni # watém bóʔó bitčáka   # 3. ʔamémak nábuhti sikáʔatek húni wéyéne 4. ínto né káá
wanting even   others road watching   with-them yonder go-if   even go-will   and I not
habem néu yahák húnii # 5. húči hoʔárau bičá   nóttibáe   ʔín áe   beu bíča #
someone to-me come even   again home-to toward return-want my mother to   toward

1. Truly this child was depending on me. It wanted to remain here and rest, I think. 2. Willing or not, I will have to wait for others, 3. to go on beyond here. 4. And even if someone comes by, 5. I am going to return again back home to my mother.

17

1. túi   ʔápoik húni # ʔápoik ím táwak húnii # 2. ʔémpo tuísi ím yépsák # 3. népo + ʔín
   all right he   just   he   here remain just   you   right here arrived myself   my
hóʔarau bíča   húči nóttibae   # 4. tá   né hunén éu híune 5. wame batóʔim nábuhti
home-to toward again return-want   but I thus to-you say-will those people beyond
katéme híba   hunáman + sékáʔana + húʔúpa   waam # hahámne ʔám téune #
travel-who always up-yonder other-side mesquite-tree there   reach-will them find

1. It's alright if he remains here. 2. You have arrived here alright. 3. I am going to return back to my home. 4. But I want to tell you, 5. those people who have gone beyond, you will reach them over at the other mesquite.

18

1. ʔéme   náwit huka + ilí   usíta + kopának + ʔámak kopánaka + nábusti aʔa núk sahakáane
   you(pl.) both that   little child rest   her-with rest   beyond   her take will
huká ilí   usíta # 2. ʔápela   sikáʔátek hunu bóʔóta au táʔaruk   3. ínto káá túʔik bítčakáʔatek
that little child   she-alone to-if   that road her get-lost-will   and not right see-if
čéa húnii + 4. ʔáʔa yóʔówem béčíibo (káá) káá tuíne   ínto béttene 5. ínto émo béčíʔibo ket
worst even   her parents for   not not good-will and heavy-will and you for   also
nókiam áma áune #
words there be-will

1. If the little child takes a rest, you both together also take a rest and take her along beyond. 2. If she goes alone she will get lost. 3. And if she sees trouble, or something worse 4. it will not be right for her parents and it will be heavy on them. 5. And people will be talking (bad) about you also.

19

1. ʔiʔánsu iníka té + mesáta betúk kátekamta háisa te túa téu wááne # 2. čúʔú ʔo wóʔí? //
now-and this we table under one-who-sits how we truly name will dog or coyote
3. ʔíni humak čúʔú bwéʔituk + 4. káá wóʔita benák bwásiak #
this maybe dog because not coyote like tail (possess)

1. Now what shall we call this one that is sitting under the table? 2. Dog or coyote? 3. Maybe this is a dog because 4. it doesn't have a tail like the coyote.

20

1. ʔilí čúʔú (aʔ) + ʔaaʔ + tekówa hum hóarápo wáiwa inéʔaka hum + béntanápo # 2. ʔáu
little dog its master in house-in inside feeling in window-at to-it
kíkteka + ʔínto čéa kia yéʔu wéyeʔ eʔámta benásiá # 3. ʔáʔa tekówa ínto wáiwa
stands and more just out go one-who-desiring like its master and inside
kíbaklataka híba káá yéu wéyebáeka bea huka ilí čúʔúta (hiba) hiókot ʔeʔétua #
entered-having always not out come-wants already that little dog always suffer feel

1. The little dog, feeling that its master is inside, is standing up at the window, 2. acting as though he wants him to come out. 3. And its master, being inside, doesn't want to come out, so is making the little dog suffer.

21

1. yán ínto ilí čúú + mesáta betúk kátekaʔú # bépa háʔamuka ilí pánim ʔo hítasa puátota
now and little dog table under sitting-was above climbing little bread or whatever plate-on
haháni # 2. wóʔókeka + ʔáma híʔíbua + 3. ʔinyé humák tebáure #
maybe scratching there eats this maybe hungry

1. And now the little dog that was under the table climbed above. There is perhaps a little bread, or something, on the plate, 2. and scratching in it, he is eating. 3. Maybe he is hungry.

22

1. ʔámali né hiáu 2. ilí čúʔú tebabáeʔure má húʔu aʔa atéakame # ʔaa míkbáeka 3. huka
right I say little dog hunger so that its one-who-owns-it it feed-wants that
puátota núʔúsek + 4. ʔíʔan intuu ilí čúʔú (buásia) buásiata yóaka áu wéyeka tuísiʔ
plate to-get now and-that little dog tail tail wagging to-it walking very
álea #
happy-is

1. I was right. 2. The little dog was hungry. So that the owner wants to feed it. 3. He is going to get the plate. 4. And now the little dog is very happy and is wagging its tail.

23

1. ʔilí (ili) čúʔúta mak násuabáeka (ʔáu) + ʔáu + mása báʔite húʔu (ilí p...) ilí palóma
little dog with fight-wanting to-itself wing fluttering the little dove
ilí čúʔú íntok + 2. ʔúnná ʔáa túʔú hiápsika bečíʔibo kiálaʔa túʔúlemčia ʔaʔa bitčú ínto
little dog and much it kind heart-being for as-if enjoying it look and
ʔáu + (ʔáu) ʔálea) #
with-it happy

1. Wanting to fight with the little dog, the little dove is fluttering its wings to him. And the little dog,
2. being of a very kind heart, is happily looking at her as though he was enjoying it.

24

1. ʔilí čúú bóe pááku tábútat   čáʔáka búʔiteka káá ʔaa haháme 2. bóetuk huʔu # tábú
   little dog great plain-in cottontail after running not to-it reach because that cottontail
čéa huni áe bépa úʔúte búíte ápo ínto háibu yumíla ínto séʔé bétte áe béčíibo + 3. tabúta
more even him over fast run he and already tired and sand heavy him for rabbit
béčíibo ínto kia séʔé ínto kia káá séʔé híba hunáen úʔúte búíte #
for and just sand and just not sand always same fast run

1. A little dog is running in a great open plain after a rabbit, and cannot reach it, 2. because the sand is heavy for the dog. And he is already tired. And the sand is very heavy for him. 3. But the rabbit, sand or no sand, always runs fast.

25

1. ʔilí čúú tábútat čáʔaka búitéka // káá a háhámeka + 2. lotíí yumúka # yeú níneka kátek
   little dog cottontail after running not it reach tired worn-out out tongue sit
íntok # 3. káá intok + aʔa haháseka intok aʔa taʔáru háksa humák aʔa kíbakekapo káá a
and not and it following and it lost where maybe he entered-where not it
húʔunéya #
know

1. A little dog, running after a rabbit, could not reach it, 2. and is worn-out tired and panting. 3. So he is not following it any more. He has lost it. He does not know which way it went.

26

1. ʔiʔán ála tiémpo túʔí + animálim bečíibo bóetuk yuʔín yúkuk síʔíme # síʔime
   now right weather good animals for because plenty rained all all
ániáči + káwim húniʔ íʔan + sía lólobóla hóʔoka 2. ínto páʔáriam into báso
world-on mountains even now green round sitting-down and plains and grass
húébena wakásim # ʔáe ʔáwine ʔíntok áe híbuane 3. ínto hipíʔikim húébenáne ímeʔe
much cattle with-it fatten-will and with-it eat-will and milk plenty-will-be these
batóʔim bečíʔibo #
people for

1. Now the weather is very good for the animals, because it rained a good deal all over the world, and the mountains are all covered with green. 2. In the plains there is plenty of grass. The cattle will eat and grow fat. 3. And there will be plenty of milk for these people.

27

1. wame batóʔim temporálim hipuéme ket hunáensu áleʔa # animálrata
   those people temporal-farms have-who also same-way happy animals (all kinds)
wélaʔapo 2. búeʔituk waʔa bém ečákaʔu buíapo bém góʔotakaʔu + síʔíme túúlisi sía # sía
besides because that they planted ground-in they thrown-have all right green green
kičíkteka hikáu wéyé 3. into kia papáʔáriam hikát čóčópoʔoku into betúktána húniʔi
coloring up coming and just plains above hills and from-below even

hunáen # ínto húya huni hunáen # ʔáu híabíttetúa hučía + táʔamak ínto báʔamak #
same and brush even same itself revive again sun-with and rain-with

1. The people who do farming by temporal, besides the animals, are very happy, 2. because what they have put under the ground is coming up in a green carpet. 3. And the plains, and the hills above and below, and the trees are reviving with the sun and water.

28

1. yán ne kéhe tua yúk táiteo ika ín kábaʔi waʔam hákun sabáanabáe báhta huébenaku
   now I not-yet truly rain start this my horse yonder where grazing-want grass where-much
yúkumak huʔu báso yuʔín tobóktila íntok # 2. ʔín kábáʔi čéʔawasu + ʔáwi lóbolái # ʔíntok +
rain-with the grass plenty risen and my horse much-more fat round and
páppéya 3. íntok ínepo huni + ʔáleáka + ʔáet náhwe ínto áet éa into áet tékipánoa #
active and I even happy-being on-it move-about and on-it use and on-it work

1. Now before it starts raining, I want to take my horse out grazing, for there is plenty of grass. The grass, with the rain, has come up high. 2. My horse is much fatter and round (like a ball), and is very active. 3. And I also ride on it happily. And I use it and work on it.

29

1. yán né béan hákun nóitebáetek húniʔ ín kábaʔi bet háʔamuk kia čúbalapo su áman
   now I want somewhere go-want-if even my horse on climb just some-(on) and yonder
ááne + 2. kía huʔu bóót + ʔilí aʔa poláktitúa íntok + ʔilí + láauti aʔa wéʔetúa
be-there-will just the road little it trot-cause-to and little slow him go-cause-to
húniʔi + čúbalápo + ʔáman 3. nóitine puéblou čéʔa + ʔó # ʔínto počóʔókun húniʔi + 4. siʔíme kut
even soon-(at) there be-will town-to more or and hills even everywhere
+ báso áuk káhíta háksa aʔa hinúriaka húniʔi + 5. ʔaʔa híʔibuatúane #
grass exists nothing where it buying even it feed-cause-will

1. Now when I want to go somewhere, I'll just get up on my horse and in a little while I'll be there. 2. Just trotting along a little on the road, and even letting him go slow, I'll be there in a little while, 3. to town or into the hills. 4. There's plenty of grass everywhere. Even if I don't buy anything for him. 5. I will see to it that he is fed.

30

1. hume náʔasom ne čéa yuʔín + čéa tutúʔim áma yéu púʔaka # 2. ʔám nénkibae + ʔabérsine
   those oranges I more better more good on out picking them sell-want to-see-if-will
ilí méliota áma náu tóhine # 3. ʔíʔi ʔéhkaléa káá túa + káá ne túa ʔa tuʔúre 4. senúk
little money on together gather-will this ladder not very not I very it like another
ne bémelak hínubáe hume náʔasom nénkakái #
I new buy-want those oranges selling

1. I am going to pick up the best oranges 2. and sell them to see if I can get a little money together out of it (them). 3. I don't like this ladder very well. 4. I am going to buy a new one after I sell these oranges.

31

1. ʔíi bakót humák wáiwa + wáitána + ʔáu metéktaita káteka itóm + ʔaa béobéoktáma
   this snake maybe inside other-side itself figure-eight-coil sitting us it flutters-its-tongue

humák + 2. ʔáiyakáme   háʔani ʔo táʔabwi bakót 3. káa té áet   húʔúnea 4. únna
maybe   one-who-has-rattles can-be or other   snake   not we no-it know   very
mékka + ʔím intóm háʔábuekaʔu ínto mékka kóʔómi ʔamán + sáhaka áʔá + bíit béčíʔibo   #
far   here we standing-where and far   down yonder   going it   see for-purpose-of
1. This snake which is on the other side has coiled up and repeatedly sticks out its tongue at us. 2. It is probably a rattlesnake or some other kind of snake. 3. We do not know what it is. 4. It is too far from here to go over and look at it.

32

1. (ket itóm) + két itóm nókáʔasu sénu ínto áu yépsák + 2. híba   túa   áiyakáme 3. bóetuk
    yet we   yet we   talk   one more to-it arrived   always truly rattlesnakes because
huʔu áiyakáme híba + híba hámúčiata núnúpne # 4. yán itépo amán + ʔím + hákíapo
the rattlesnakes always always female bring-will   now we yonder   here canyon-in
ʔáwe? kóom káteka wáitána # sahákáʔatek amán (am) + ʔám núʔúka + ʔám yéam tóhiʔéan
could down going other-side go-if   yonder   them take   them out carry-could
amán hakúnsa bém híhínu wáawi ʔó itépo + ʔám atéaʔéan #
yonder where they buy   where or we   they own-could
1. Just as we were talking, there arrived another one. 2. I think it is a rattlesnake, 3. because a rattlesnake always has a female with him. 4. Now if we could climb down these cliffs, we could go to the other side to get them and take them where we could sell them, or we could keep them (ourselves).

33

1. iʔán íntuči   humee bakóčim áʔabo itóm háriú # 2. ʔitó ʔam bítbáeo íntok + bémposu bimá
   now and-again those snakes here us search   we them see-want and   they-and this
botána tóm anéʔe béas   itóm + ʔááneka itóm góómtaka číbela   itóm náíkim hahásuk
side íwe are on-the-path our is-staying us frightening scattered-have us apart chased
3. ité ínto ám + ʔúnna ʔám huuʔéna tíaka káa ámeu rúktibáeka ʔám tóʔtó ténnek #
    we and them   much them dangerous saying not to-them approaching them left ran
1. And now the snakes came on this side to search for us. 2. Since we wanted to see them, they came over to this side and were on our path. They frightened all of us and we ran and scattered all over the place. They chased us all over, 3. and we said they were very dangerous. We didn't approach them, but ran away from them.

34

1. táʔata yéu wéyeo neʔ + bááwanámak lópola wéyeamáka (ili) + ʔilí kanóata + wóim
   sun out going I   sea-shore   alongside going-beside   little canoe   two
bélakámta # 2. ʔáa bitčáka ínto # batóʔim ne + káá habém ʔa bitča 3. humak áápela weáma húʔu
sails-with   it saw   and people I not some it see   perhaps alone travel the
ilí + bóte ʔó + únna + káá mamáčisi emo hóala humee hábeʔesáim aʔa núnuʔubwáme #
little boat or much   not visible they sitting those whoever it drive-who
(humee) + 4. ʔinto káá + ʔúʔúte bóʔo hóa íntok + káá hekámak bóʔo hóamta benásia má čéa +
           and not   fast road make and   not wind-with road making like so more
wásala   hum báʔapo wéye #
crossways on water-on travel
1. At sunrise (*lit.* sun-coming-out) I was walking along side the seashore and I saw a little boat with two sails. 2. And I did not see anybody inside the boat. 3. Perhaps the little boat is traveling alone or perhaps

the people who are driving it are hiding themselves from sight. 4. It does not travel with the wind but is going crossways.

35

1. túa tá?ata áman wéčeo ínto + bááwenámak + lópola # 2. ?úsi hámút wáki bwíapo wé?eka
    truly sun yonder falling and sea-shore beside child female dry earth-on standing
húka + remó bótepo + ó?óuta yésiménta # ?a?a bitčú hú?u 3. ínto + ?ó?óu ínto + húka +
that oar boat-on man sitting it looking the and man and that
remóta tobóktaka áu hikáu + ?áu á?a so?isó?ita 4. háisa húmak áu híubáeka hu?u ?úsi
oar raising to-her up to-her it raise-raise what may to-her say-want the child
hámuttáwi # 5. hu?u ?úsi hámut ínto kááčin húni? ááne kía túa áman a?a bitčú # 6. hu?u tá?a
female the child female and not-any even doing just truly yonder it look the sun
béa túa áman wéči?ise + ?iním + oráapo #
already truly yonder falling this hour-at

1. Actually, at sunset [*lit.* sun-yonder-falling] beside the seashore, 2. a girl stands on dry ground and looks at the man sitting in the rowboat. 3. The man on the boat is raising the oar and waving it to her. 4. Whatever he wants to say, I don't know. 5. The girl does not make any gestures, but just keeps looking. 6. The sun, by this hour, is just going down.

36

1. yoéme úsi hámúttamak + wéyéka tá?ata áman wéčeo # (báawemak lópola katéka + ?im) +
    man child female-with walking falling sea-with alongside walking here
báawemak lópola katéka + ?im + 2. nórteu bičá náu bó?o hóa tá + hu?u ó?óu kía
sea-with alongisde walking here north-to toward together road doing but the man just
áu ?ómtemta benási 3. ?amáu a?a tó?o símlataka káá áu bitčú ínto kía # 4. káá amak
to-her angry like back her leave went not to-her look and just not with-her
etého húni?i # 5. téa bésa bém sáhaka?u hábe hú?únea #
speak even but already they going no-one know

1. A man is walking with a girl at sundown alongside the sea. 2. They are traveling toward the north but the man looks as though he is angry with her, 3. so he is leaving her behind and does not even look at her, 4. nor talk to her. 5. But where they are going nobody knows.

37

1. ?iním ne ná?aso soyó?oku yépsák humak órtelánotau + ?ime ná?ásom netáneka 2. ?ám
    here I orange grove arrive maybe orchard-keeper-to these oranges beg-for them
púaka ?ám núk saká?atek ?ám púataka ?ám núk siká hóarata ?ám nonó?atek 3. két né huma
picking them take go-if them loading them take going home them peddle-if yet I might
ám nénkaka ilí méliota áma bítne # 4. téa ne bésa huka órtelánota káá im láutipo
them selling little money there see-will but I already that orchard-keeper not here presently
bitčá humák káábe há?ani #
see maybe no-one be-here-would

1. If I come to this orchard, this grove, if I ask the orchard keeper for these oranges, 2. if I can pick them up, and if I take them upon my shoulder and take them away and peddle them around the houses, 3. maybe I can make a little money out of it. 4. But I don't see the orchard keeper now, and he might not be around here.

38

(sun) 1. súúnta ne siálik + kaméyon yá'apo há'ábukámta kée + kéé + bakámta # bitčú
      corn I green   furrows made-in stands-which not   not   green-corn-on see
2. téa bésa   huma čé'a waam héela háisa máisi + báčita itóm máknekái # 3. hu'u á'a atéakame
   but already might more yonder a-little some how   corn us give-will   the it owns-who
tuísi a'a súaé ínto nákeka á'a bitčá + káábeta áma kíkimútúa íntok kía # hábeta húnii káa
well it care and loves it see   no-one there go-in-allows and just no-one even not
'áma + náhwéye   áu 'áa' étpo # 4. 'ápo 'a'a tú'ute ínto bičá á'a bá'atúa íntok #
there about-walks to-it his plant-in   he it   clean and toward it waters and
5. sényórta betána két yúkú áet kó'om wéye #
   the-Lord from   also rain on-it down fall

1. I am looking at some green plants of corn planted in furrows, but it has not borne any fruit yet. 2. A little later it might give us some corn. 3. The owner does not let anybody go inside, and just doesn't let anybody walk over his plants. 4. He cleans it up and he waters it and he takes care of it. 5. And also from the Lord the rain comes down upon it.

39

1. 'iním humák óri   + hume báto'im wa'am saháka'apo iní humák hunuén óri   + dragún
   here maybe I-think those people by   went   this might thus I-think Dragoon
téa   2. bóetuk inépo ket wókim méa iniét wa'am símla + 3. 'inime kábuim   ne am tá'áya
named because myself also foot on here by   went   these mountains I them know
bóetuk ne + húébenasi 'ám bítla íntok 4. humák + tá'abui húmakú'u téa bésa # hunále benási
because I many-times them seen and   maybe   other   might but alright them like
kía mamáči hu'u ánia 5. hu'u páária into hu'u popóčui íntok hu'u + béntéme #
just seems the world the plain   and the hills and the foothills

1. I think this is the place where the people went by, and I think the name of the place is Dragoon, 2. because I went by here on foot. 3. The mountains I know well because I have been through here so many times, and I have seen those mountains. 4. It might be another place, but it looks very much like the area, 5. the plains, the hills, and the mountains and foothills.

40

1. 'iníí yoéme íntok + náwit a'a + mámbetá'im itóm bíbíttúame kía hunén itóm tetééhoámta
   this man and   both his   hand-palms us shows-who just thus us tells
2. benáh kómo yó'ówem itóu híhíusuka'apo benásia ín mámpo e'e 'áma yóek + 'i'áni tía #
   like as   elders us-to told-have where like my hand-in you out escape now says
3. 'a'a yópna   into hunén áu hía + (káá) káá áma yóeká'atek húni'i kía mámpo 'áma
   him answering and thus to-it say   not not there escape-it   even   just hand-in there
yó'ekti   kía áu hiúne í'an 4. íntok # 'iní ó'óu ket a'a mámbetá'im itóm bíbíttúaka hunen itóm
escaped-so just to-it saying now and   this man also his hand-palms us showing thus us
a'a hú'unéyatúa #
it known-make

1. This man is showing us the palm of his hands, (this man) who seems to be telling us, 2. as our elders used to tell us, "You have just escaped out of my hands." 3. And in answer to him the other said, "If I escape at all I will only barely escape out of your hands." 4. And now this man is showing us the palms of his hands.

41

1. ʔián ínto humeʔ + ʔáu úúbaka (ma) máman káá wačáʔika kóʔom bičá ʔam buísaka 2. kía
   now and those   himself wash   hands not drying   down toward them holding just
kála (kála) číháčihakti kóʔom huʔu báʔa čákteka # 3. kóom mámam čáʔári mám pusiámpo kóom
clean   splashing down the water dropping   down hands   hanging hand fingers-on down
bičá   kia tatábúhtiata benási áet kóʔom wéye huʔu + báʔá #
toward just heat-sweat like   on-it down go   the   water

1. And now after he has washed himself without drying off his hands he is hanging them down 2. and the water is coming down in clear drops. 3. As his hands hang down the water comes down through his fingers like sweat.

42

1. hámút yóʔówe + mesáta bépa húmak + hukáʔa + híʔík wáata tóʔó siká 2. íntok # ʔimeʔe
   woman old   table-on upon maybe   the   needle basket left went and   these
híʔíkiam ínto omót   hóʔárika 3. ínto + ʔínwain mesápo huka híʔik wáata mánekámta háiwa
needles and elsewhere placed   and   hither table-on the needle basket stands   searching
tá ʔíntok húʔu áma wáatewame   ínto kahíta ʔáma áuk # 4. humak + húʔú + táʔabwi aʔa
but and   the there wanted-what-is and nothing there exist maybe   the   other it
úsiwa   hábesa humak yéu + ʔómotta bičá   núk siká hunéʔelaka áma mánek húʔu híʔik
child-her someone maybe out elsewhere toward took went empty   there stand the needle
wáʔari #
basket

1. The old lady probably left her needle basket on top of the table. 2. And as for the needles, she must have also placed them somewhere else. 3. She came up here to the table to search for the needle basket, but what she wants in the basket is not there. 4. Probably a child or somebody has taken it out and left the basket empty.

43

1. tá   huléntak húniʔi + hukaʔa híʔík wáata hunéʔelaka hume mesápo núʔuk aʔa núk síika #
   but anybody even   that   needle basket empty   table-on grasped it took went
2. ʔamán aʔa + kátékau bičá huniʔi humák amáni hákun   humák híʔíkiam aʔa kóptalapo
   yonder she sitting toward even maybe yonder somewhere maybe needles it   forgotten-where
hunáman téune háʔani teʔéwapo benásia 3. tá bésa káá húʔunéiya túa lutúla wéʔepo #
yonder find-will might as-thought like   but already not know   truly straight going
(háksáhi) + 4. háksumeʔe híʔíkiam ínto humeʔe táhoʔota aa tóó sikápo   #
              where-those needles and those clothes   it left went-where

1. But anyway, she took the empty needle basket and carried it away 2. toward where she had been sitting before. Perhaps out yonder where she had been sitting she had forgotten the needles, and (it is) as though she were hoping perhaps to find the needles there. 3. But already she does not know exactly where she left those needles. 4. Nor does she know where she left those clothes (patches).

44

1. ʔííʔ ínto óʔóu im + mesáta bépa húka + kúh kutáta + tóó siká 2. intiʔán ínto humee
   this and man here   table-on upon this   cross wood   left went   and-now and those

nabáʔásom hume kúusim áe   aʔa kutúktaneʔu (káá) + káá téktéaka 3. kia húka kúh kutáta híba
blades   that rosary   with-it it carve-will   not finding   just that cross wood just
ama bepa tékika # 4. ʔaʔa bítčuka   áet amán weámak ínto humeʔe nabáʔásom ínto háiwa   #
there upon laid   it looking on-it yonder walk   and those   blades   and searching
1. This man has laid the rosary wood on top of the table, 2. and now he cannot find the knife with which he carves the beads, 3. but he has just laid the wood there (on top of the table), 4. and he is moving around looking at it. He is also searching for the knife.

45

1. humeʔe kúčiʔim + (kúčiʔim) káá húʔunéiyaka húniʔi híba   hum mesáta bépa kúh kutáta
    this knife   not knowing   even always there table upon cross wood
bóokamta núʔuka # ʔaʔa núk síika hume # 2. ʔían ínto hume nabáʔasom besa háriútáitek 3. beha ʔó
lays-which took · it took went this   now and this knife   just search-began   just or
ʔam téune + ʔó káá ʔam téune 4. tá beha ʔápo ala huka kutáta wéíya # ʔáe kúúsim
them find-will or not them find-will but already he   then that wood carrying with-it crosses
hóawámta #
made-up
1. Not even knowing the whereabouts of the knife he took with him the rosary wood which was laying on top of the table. 2. And now he has started searching again for the knife. 3. He may find it or he may not find it. 4. The fact is that he carried away the wood from which the rosaries are made.

46

1. wói batóim émo   famíliaka # wóim úseka   sénu ilí óʔóu sénu ínt ili hámút #
   two people each-other family-having two children-having one little boy one and little girl
2. ʔám pásealóatúabáekai   yéuámnúksáhak   háisa bem ʔám nakíʔéya béčíʔibo # 3. ʔim
   them walk-to-cause-desiring out-them-take-going how they them love-feel for   here
mámpo ʔam bwísaka ʔam súʔaé hítasa   káá + ʔámeu čáʔatuneʔe 4. béčiʔibo ínto bémpo
hand-by them holding them care something not to-them happen   for   and themselves
káá omón háksa yéu ténnéka hitása   ámet   bwítine bečíʔibo mámpo ʔam buísaka ʔám
not one-side where out running something to-them run-will for   hand-by them holding them
wéíyea # 5. ʔápo óʔóu íntok húʔú # huʔu hámút (huʔu ilí óʔot) + huʔu ilí óʔóuta nasúk aʔa
taking   he man and the   the woman   the little boy between him
wéyeaka ilí hamútta ínto # bátatána mámpo hámúta áʔa + buísime mámpo # ʔáʔa súʔaé béčíʔibo #
taking little girl and right-side hand-at woman it holding hand-by   her care for
1. Two people have each other as family and have two children, one a little boy and the other a little girl. 2. Desiring to take them out for a walk because they love them so much, 3. they are leading them and holding them by the hand in order to watch them and to avoid anything happening to them, 4. for they might run to one side or something might run over them. 5. He, the man, and the woman are leading them holding them by the hand. The little boy is being led between them and the little girl is being led by the woman.

47

1. íním ála béha (hántiaček) + hántiaček hákiáta sibáta mékka kóʔómikú # (há) 2. náu
   here now really frightful   frightful canyon cliff far   down where   together
háʔabweka mékka náu   + ʔétehóka íntok + káá túa émo   híkkáha kía hukaa kukúpapámta
standing far together talking and   not truly each-other hearing just that echo

híba híkkáʔaka # háʔabuek 3. íntok kááčin náu   ánmačí kia káá náu   rúkte ínto kia káá
just hearing   standing   and   not-how together getting just not together   approach and just not
ʔémo   + tuísi húni nók híkkáha # 4. ʔínto huʔu síba áma béa bútti hántiaček mékka kóʔomi
each-other   well even talk approach   and the cliff there over much frightfully far   down
áman kóʔom saháka náu   yáhi béčíʔibo #
yonder down going together arrive far

1. It is really frightful, the cliffs and the canyon, way down deep. 2. The men are standing on either side and they are talking to each other and they don't hear each other. They are just standing and they can only hear the echo of the words. 3. And they cannot get together and they cannot approach each other and don't hear each other very well. 4. The canyon is so deep it is impossible to go down and meet.

48

1. ʔíʔan ínto waʔa + sénu óri + wáitána betána wéʔekámta # huʔu hámút + ʔáu   yépsáka #
   now and that   one   then   other-side from standing-who the woman   to-him came
2. huʔu sénu ínto ámeú   nóóka tá káá ámeú   kúsiata nóóka 3. má čéam kía háʔabweka áʔa
   the one and to-them talk but not to-them heard talk   so that just standing him
bitčú íʔi nás aʔa mám áo   # ʔaʔa + nóókiwa kía huni + nás   aʔa mámap híba ilí áet
looking this about him hand moving his words just even about him hand-in just little to-it
húʔu nakiáči # 4. ʔian intúči   húka sibáta maháika káá ámeu   rúkteka háčin húni káá
that obvious   now and-again this cliff   fearing not to-them approach how even not
émo   + túʔute máči nókpo #
each-other   arrange clearly word-by

1. Now a woman came to the one who is standing on the other side and 2. the one on this side is talking to them, but they don't hear each other. 3. It appears that the others are just standing on the other side and don't hear what he is saying, the way he is gesticulating with his hands. They understand only a little by the way he is moving his hands. 4. And now again, since they are afraid of these frightful cliffs and since they cannot approach each other, they cannot make any arrangement by speaking.

49

1. huka senúk huka hámútta áʔa tóʔó sik # (ket) + két hunén hiúwá # su iʔí   botána + biná
   that one that woman   him left went   yet thus saying then this side   from
botána wéyekame ápela batnátaka áma ʔanéú yán huʔu sénu hámút áu   yepsáka # 2. ʔinto
this-side stands-who alone at-first there were now the one woman to-him arriving   and
áʔa + temá   3. hitása émpo ámeu nóóka hume wáitána háʔabwekámeu 4. néhpo béha #
him questioning what you(sg.) them-to say those other-side stand-who-to   I   already
humák bémpoim aman nókau káá ám híkkáha # 5. ʔémpo ínto híba   hunún wéyéka ámet
perhaps them yonder talking on them hear   you(s.) and always there stand them-to
čáe   + 6. kía mékka kukúpapa huʔu eʔém čáeʔú   #
yelling   just far   echo   that you yelling-to

1. As we were saying, the woman left the man on the other side and another woman came to the other man who was at first standing alone on this side, 2. and she has started questioning him, 3. "What are you saying to those people who are standing on the other side? 4. I myself cannot hear a word that they are saying. 5. And you are standing there just hollering to them. 6. Just the echo is heard a long way."

50

1. bát á?á nú?úkame á?á atéane tiámta benási 2. ika + tómita + buíapo + téaka # ?áu
   first it pick-who it own-will saying-who like this money earth-on finding to-it
kó?om pó?oktek 3. hu?u sénu ínto kía kúrik kóbaka a?a bítčuk 4. íntok # humák káá ?álea 5. káá
down stooped the one and just wrinkle head it look and might not feel-well not
apó bát á?a tobóktakai huka tómita buíapo wéčeata #
he first it pick-up-have that money earth-on fallen

1. As the saying goes, "The one who picks it up first is the owner" (*e.g.* "finders keepers"). 2. Finding this money, the man stooped down to pick it up. 3. The other man looks on with a wrinkled forehead. 4. He might be feeling bad because 5. he did not first pick up the money which was on the ground.

POSITIONALS AND DIRECTIONALS TEXT

1

1. ?i?íbwan sénú yoéme (?ilí) + ?ilí puétata étapóka hum + káriwi + kíbakekai puétata étapoik tá
   this one man little door opening there house entered door opened but
bitčáka íntok # ket káá áman kíbakeka 2. ínto hum béntanaú kíkteka áman # túisi
seeing and yet not there enter and there window-at standing yonder much
bitčúsuka íntuči # 3. húči nótteka huka puétata + étapóka áman ínto puétapo wéeka
looked-in-having and-again again return that door opening yonder and door-at standing
áman wáiwa bičá bitčú iáni #
yonder inside toward looking now

1. This one man went through the gate, went to the front of the house, opened the door, but he didn't go inside. 2. (He went) around to the window and looked through the window into the house. 3. He turned back around, went to the front of the house, opened the door, and is standing in front of it looking inside.

2

1. puétata étapoka áman wáiwa bitčúk ínto húči káata kóntaka + (?ín) + ?íntuči áman
   door opening there inside looking and again house circled and-again yonder
nótteka huká? hum # puétapo wéyeka 2. káá nóoka ínto kía hábe húni?i hum kári wáiwa
returning that there door-at standing not talking and yet anybody even there house inside
betána káábe a?a yóayópna 3. ?intááp íntok + káá hú?únéa hitási humák a?a wáatá?u ?ó ?a?a
from no-one him answer and-he and not know what maybe he want or it
hú?unéayéa + 4. ?í?án + te béha ápoik temáetek híba hú?unéne #
know now we already him question-if always know-will

1. He opened the door and looked inside and then again he went (all the way) around the house and stood in front of the door. 2. (He) doesn't say anything, nor does anybody from inside the house talk to him or answer him. 3. And now perhaps he doesn't know what he wants. Maybe he does or not. 4. And now, we'll have to question him if we are going to know what he wants.

3

1. pá?ákun yéu nóitéka + kúhtaú séhtul nóitéka # íntúči + 2. húči nótteka íntúči + bemélasi
   outside out went cross-to once went and-again again return and-again anew

húči   nótteka hum puétau íʔan kíktek intúči # 3. náh   bitčú tá   káábe hum ket tebátpo ínto kía
again return   now door   now stands again   around look but no-one there yet yard-in and just
wáiwa huni káábeta bitčú #
inside even no-one see

1. He went outside and stood before the cross. 2. He returned and again he returned. And now he stands in front of the door. 3. He does not see anybody in the patio (or the yard), and he does not see anybody inside.

4

1. ʔiʔán ínto káá símbáeka   hum + kááta   + buíkola hiba náh   wéwélta íntok # 2. ramáau
   now and not go-wanting there   house-to around just about circling and   ramada-to
séhtul nóitek íntuči   (húči) hum puéta betána kíkteka # 3. kía kúhta bičá   puséka wéyeka
once went and-again again there door from standing   just cross-at toward eyes-with stands
+ káá nóóka íntuči   + 4. íntása   humák # amá hóasísíme # 5. ʔáʔa bitčáme híba húʔunéne #
  not talking and-again   and-what maybe there doing   him see-who only know-will

1. And now he does not want to go away. He's just going around the house, circling it. 2. And he went to the ramada once, then came back to the side where the door is. 3. He's standing there looking at the cross, and he doesn't say anything. 4. Again we don't know what he's doing there. 5. Except by looking at him you can almost guess what he's doing.

5

1. bóetuk hum nóókpo + káábe áet   húʔunéne ápo híta húni kía téuwa 2. ínto kia čúʔú húni
   because there word-in   no-one on-it know-will he thing even yet said   and just dog even
káábe hum hóʔarápo 3. ínto húʔu # kúhtaú húni káa múhte   4. íntok + ramáata betuk húni
no-one there house-at   and the   cross-to even not genuflection and   ramada-at under even
kée   kíbakek íán # 5. kía húka kááta híba   túa súámta benási + ʔáma ʔááne #
not-yet go-in   now   just that house always truly guard same-as there doing

1. Except by his words no one can know what he wants, and he hasn't said anything. 2. There is not even a dog at the household. 3. He has not done a genuflexion to the cross, 4. and he has not been under the ramada yet. 5. He's really acting as though he were just guarding the house.

6

1. ʔián béha   húka + kárita túa napéčikóla ʔaʔa wéltasúla ʔóʔóben tá ne káá húʔunéa ket huniʔi
   now already that   house truly clear-around it   circled   it's-true but I not know   yet even
hítasa humák nókobáe káá nóóka híba   hunéni # 2. ʔian intúči   nóttek huʔu kááta amáu betána
what might talk-want not talk always how   now and-again return that house back-to side
siká + hikáu + ʔáet   háʔamuka + íʔan kía óri kúsísia áet   bépa hikát weáma hum káriči
went   up   upon-it climb   now then ah noisy   upon-it over up   walk there house-on
áma húniʔi # 3. né híkkáʔatek hotéʔine + hotéka yéu sakáʔane hume batóʔim wáiwa aneme
there even   me hearing   rise   if-rise out come-will those people inside exist-who
tiámta   bénásia #
as-one-would-say like

1. Now he has gone clear around the house, but I do not know yet what he might want to say. He does not say anything yet. 2. And now he returned again toward the back of the house and climbed on top of it. 3. And he is walking above the house making a noise. "Maybe if they hear me they will get up and come out, the people who are inside."

7

1. ʔíʔan (ínto) ínto tatáriata áu húiwatúaka? + hum + ramáata betúkun kíbakek kía into
   now and and heat to-himself feels that ramada under entered just and
   túa ama bóʔoka # 2. kía áman áu hoʔále ían čéʔa #
   truly there lying just there to-himself home now worst

1. Now after he had stopped walking around the house he felt hot and went into the ramada, and is now lying down 2. as if he considered the place his own home.

8

1. ínto ramáapo bóʔo(lo)téka páʔakun bičá yéu siká túa ilí kóra éskinápo # kía wéyéka #
   and ramada-in lying outside toward out went truly little fence corner-on just standing
2. ʔáman + hikáu aʔa bitčúka + kórata únná mékka hikáči kóra čépta béčíibo tiámta bénásia #
   yonder up it looking fence-the very far up fence jump for saying like

1. After he was tired of lying down under the ramada, he got up and went to the corner of the fence. And just standing 2. he stared at it as if he were saying, "The corral is too high to jump over."

9

1. kórata káá ʔáa čéptaka iʔan ínto beha túa + túa húʔúnakteka hum # 2. káriwi wáiwa kía
   fence not it jumping now and already truly truly intention there house-to inside just
   káá lisénsiaka áman kíbakek ían íntok # 3. ʔáma + humak ápo wáiwa bóʔoka humák ramáapo +
   not permission there went now and there there he inside lying maybe ramada-at
   káá ínto bóʔobáekai #
   not more lie-wanting

1. After he tried to jump over the fence and couldn't make it, (and after lying under the ramada), 2. he went inside the house. 3. Perhaps he is inside lying down, not wanting to lie down in the ramada anymore.

10

1. ʔáhta ían húʔúbwa húmaku batóe ʔéak máčéa ían kúhtaú kíkteka áman + ʔáu +
   until now just maybe baptism feeling seems now cross-at standing there to-himself
   líonóoka ʔó ʔáu kúhte ʔo ʔáu múhte # 2. nuuká ne káá húʔunéya bóetuk mékka hum
   blessing or to-it (sign of cross) or to-it bowing-head that I not know because far there
   in wéʔeka ʔaa bítčúpo # 3. híba túa áu líonóok bóetuk ʔían + wáéhma au buanía
   I stand him look-where just truly to-himself pray because now Lent himself blessing
   hiókoči húmakúʔu #
   with-great-effort maybe

1. At this moment he has perhaps remembered his baptism so he has stood before the cross to pray and bow to the cross. He has thought about the love of God. 2. The way I look at him, not knowing exactly what he is doing, 3. he's probably praying for himself because the time is now Lent.

11

1. huʔu kúseu líonóoksuka íntok + kíkteka # 2. hum kári éskináu + wéʔeka húči + náh
   the cross-to prayed-having and stood-up here house corner standing again about
   bitčú # 3. hakún bičása humák kuáktiné káá íʔani + nábúhti bičá #
   looking where toward-to might turn-about-will not now beyond toward

1. After having prayed to the cross, 2. now he stands up there at the corner of the house, and looks around. 3. Which way he will turn from here I don't know.

12

1. ʔíʔan intim ramáata púntapo wéeka yén táitek 2. íʔan íntok kia (kiuka) huka ramáata
    now and-here ramada end-at standing smoke started now and just this ramada
huni táiyáʔana kia éwači 3. bóetuk huʔu ramáa kia sánkoa áusúʔuli # 4. kia híta ilí táhi
even burn-will just believed because the ramada just dry-brush pure just any little fire
áet wéček húni aʔa táiyáʔane #
on-it fall even it burn-will

1. And now, standing at the end of the ramada, he has started smoking. 2. There is a risk he will burn the ramada 3. since a ramada is only dry brush. 4. Just any spark falling on it will start a fire.

13

1. hunuén + ʔiʔi ramáat + hikáu háʔamuka káá ilí sánkoa áusúʔuli kia húči ʔían 2. ínto
    so-thus this ramada-on up-to climbing not little dry-brush pure just again now and
hikát káteka # yéna háisa humaku ʔo ʔaa táiyáʔane ʔo + (ʔo) húʔúnakteku táiyáʔabáeka 3. hunen
on-tip sitting smoke how perhaps or it burn-will or intentionally burn-wants thus
áane ápola hikát káteka yéna #
doing he on-top sitting smoke

1. And so climbing above this ramada which is purely dry brush, 2. he is sitting on top smoking. I don't know, but he might be doing this intentionally, in order to burn it. 3. So he is sitting on top of the ramada smoking.

14

1. ʔiʔan íntuči hum ramáapo kóʔóm čépteka # betúk íʔan náh wéyekasu # 2. tuá tebát
    now and-again there ramada-on down jump under now about walks truly yard-in
násuk wéʔeka # ʔíntuči + hitása + huma yáʔabae 3. tá káá mónte húči hita káíta nóókta
middle standing and-again what might do-want but not saying again thing nothing word
kée ʔáet híkkáha #
not-yet on-it hear

1. And now jumping from the ramada, he walks below. 2. Actually he is standing in the middle of the yard, and again I don't know what he wants to do. 3. He's not said a word yet, not a word which I have heard from him.

15

1. ʔíʔan ínto čéʔa ama áu hóʔatek 2. má čéa huká + puétata páttáika 3. áma kia wáiwa +
    now and worse there himself home-if so worse that door-at closed there just inside
yántelá # páʔákum bičá bitčúk wéyek #
at-ease outside toward looking standing

1. He may even think that he lives there now, 2. so he closed the door. 3. He stands there inside and looks out.

16

1. ʔían íntok hum ramáata betúkun + kia áman nóiteka húči nótteka # 2. hum + kóra puétau
   now and there ramada under just there going again returning there fence gate-to
   wéeka # 3. páʔariau bíča náh bitčú kúhta bičápo #
   standing plain-to toward about looking cross-at facing-there

1. And now he is just coming and going back and forth to the ramada, and returning again to the fence gate. 2. He is standing there in front of the cross 3. looking outside toward the plains.

17

1. ʔíʔan ála béa híta ama étbwabáe hum káripo má čéa hum béntanápo ʔamáni
   now then already what there steal-wanting there house-in so much there window-in through
   kíbakeka # 2. ʔían káá ʔamán + mamáči hitása humak # nasónte ʔo ʔétbwa ʔo ʔaa túʔúte ʔó háisa
   entered now not there visible what might destroying or stealing or it fixing or what
   hóʔa #
   doing

1. Now, I think he wants to steal something in the house, so he is climbing in through the window. 2. There inside what he might be doing is invisible (to us), whether he may be destroying, or stealing or fixing, or whatever doing.

18

1. káá hítasa huma ama núʔúka má čéa hum sékaʔana béntanau im táʔata yéu wéeʔ (táʔata yéu
   not anything maybe there take so there next window here sun out going
   wée) betána # kátekámtaʔa # 2. ʔamá yeú sikaá ʔínto + húči páʔaka wéʔeka náh bitčú #
   from sits-the-one-who there out went and again outside standing about looking
   3. tá kahíta híta mačúʔute ínto kia bóusapo kimáʔika wéyeamta bena máčeʔa + hunéʔela #
   but nothing thing holding and just pocket-in inside walks like so bare

1. He did not take anything maybe. And he went to the window which is toward the sunrise. 2. He came outside again and he is standing there looking around. 3. He is not holding anything in his hands, and I think he doesn't have anything in his pockets.

19

1. níí yoéme káá námukíataka íntok hunuén hum hóarapo wáiwa kórapo ʔánsísime 2. tá # káá
   this man not drunk-being and that-way there home-at inside fence-in doing but not
   hábee humák hum hóarapo hóʔóka 3. máčea káá áu + yéu réhtek ʔáu nóóka ʔó mékka aʔa
   person maybe there home-at exist seems not to-him out come to-him talk or away him
   béba húniʔi #
   send even

1. This man, though not being drunk, is acting that way in this house inside the fence. 2. Maybe there's no one at the place 3. and that's why no one comes out and talks to him, or even sends him away.

20

1. ʔíʔan ala íntuči hum káriu kíbakeka # túísi hum písopo kúsisi náh wéye 2. humák
   now then and-again there house-to went very there floor-on loud about walk might
   káítasan káapo wáiwa áuk 3. má čéa kíaʔ + ʔáman náh wéwóltamta benási kúsisi wéye áman

nothing house-in inside exist   so   just   there about circling   as-though loud go   there
+ wóko písopo #
lumber floor-on

1. Now then he goes inside the house and walks on the floor making a loud noise. 2. And there might be nothing in the house. 3. So it seems he is going around in circles on the wooden floor making a loud noise.

21

1. ʔían íntok + huma ama náh wéyesuka hum káʔapo wáiwa ínto hukaʔa kárita pátták ʔó +
now and   maybe there about walked-having there house-in inside and that   house closed or
húʔúnakteka ʔáu   pátták ʔó háisa   # 2. ʔáp aʔaʔ + ʔéapo ʔaʔa páttáika áma káá yéu wéye ʔían
intentionally himself closed or whatever   he his   will-in it   closed   there not out walk now
íntokó #
and

1. Now after having walked inside of the house he closed the door, and he may have closed himself inside intentionally. 2. He determined to close it, and now he doesn't want to come out.

22

1. puétata ála étapóka óʔoben   tá   bea   into káá yéu weáma háisa humák + húme
door   is opening nevertheless but already and not out walk   what might
áulátakái # 2. kia + puéta étapóittu óʔoben   kóra puétau bičá   bitčúka ʔama wéyek hum
having-been   just   door opened   nevertheless fence gate-to toward looking there stand there
wáiwa #
inside

1. He opened the door but he nevertheless doesn't want to walk out. Whatever might have happened 2. the door is open and he is standing inside looking toward the gate.

23

1. ʔíʔan ála   páʔakun yéu sikáa ʔíntok húči hum # 2. kóra puétau bičá   + wééka   + náh
now then outside out went and again there   fence gate-to toward   standing   about
bítčú #
looking

1. And now, coming outside there, 2. he goes toward the fence gate and stands there looking about.

24

1. yán ínto hun + wáata sánta kúhta čáʔapao   + ʔilí sewátau kíkteka áman # ket áʔa
now and there   willow holy cross below-where   little flower-to stands yonder   also it
bitčúk káá humak + ʔaʔa babáʔ atúawa tíaka ilen nóóka # 3. sánta kús   into bépa síalika +
looking not maybe   it   water give   says thus talks   holy cross and above green
wéyek #
standing

1. And now, standing where the holy cross hangs, he stands and stares at a little flower. 2. He thought, "Maybe they do not water it." Thus he talks. 3. And a holy willow cross stood above.

25

1. ʔinépo čéʔa kía aʔa náwi ʔéyan   + 2. kia ʔiʔán čeʔa kia ilí   úsita + benási + čóʔaktekai
I   more just it sissy thought   just now more just little child   like   frolicking

huka kórata + mékka hikáči káá ilí   aa? tubúktaka # 3. ?í?an ínto + hum + séka?ana wáitan
that fence   far   up   not little it jumping   now and   there   other   otherside
wéyeka + hum + hóarau bítču # 4. káábeta áma téakai #
standing   there   house-to looking   nobody there found

1. I myself thought him just to be a sissy and 2. now, more as though he were a little child frolicking, he jumped over the fence which is very high. 3. Now he stands on the other side looking toward the house, 4. but finds no one there.

26

1. ?ían čé?a huma + čé?awásu ?ama ?áu   ho?ále 2. má čeá kia + hume kútam + náu
  and more maybe   worse   there his-own home   so more just those sticks   together
tóhaka # tú?úlisia móola nát   ?am mónto # 3. náiya?abáemta benásia tá + into + humak hume +
carry   nicely pile top-on them piling   burn-wants like but and might those
báhi ibáktim + káá hwébena + 4. má čéa? ama wéyeka ?amán bitču + húči 5. humak + ?am
three armfuls not enough   so more there standing yonder looking again might them
púabae   hume?e kútam #
pickup-want those   sticks

1. And even worse, he now believes that he lives there, 2. so he is carrying the wood and piling it in a nice pile 3. as though he might want to build a fire, but maybe the three armfuls are not enough. 4. So he is standing there looking yonder again. 5. Maybe he wants to pick up some more wood.

27

1. kútam náu   tóhisúka íntok + ?ámeu bičá # kórau amáka yéhték + 2. ?í?an íntok hitása
  wood together carried and   to-them toward fence back-with sit   now and   what
humak káá ?ám + náiyaabae 3. íntok kia káá ?am + wéiyaabáe 4. íntok kia káá ínto húni +
might not them   fire-want   and just not them carry-want   and just not and even
náu   ?am tóhibáe hume watém + kía číbela   wó?otílam #
together them carry-want those others   just scattered fallen

1. After having gathered the wood, he sat with his back against the fence, in front of the wood. 2. And now it might be that he doesn't want to build a fire, 3. nor does he want to carry it (the wood) away, 4. nor does he want to gather any more of the dry wood which is scattered on the ground.

28

1. ?ían íntuka puétata + ?ápo míhmo + ?a?a páttáika ínto káá?a tetéaka # 2. hu?u kóramak
  now and-this gate   he himself   it closed   and not-it find   the fence-with
lópola weáma rébe kía hume ilí kúta pupú?imét + ?áu   bwí?ibwí símeka + 3. ?í?an ínto
alongside walking partly just those little wood sharp-on   himself holding goes   now and
hum(e) kútam a?a móntóipo # hum ama éskinapo lúula wé?ek + 4. tá # ket húni + kée
there wood it piled-where there there corner-at straight stands   but yet even   not-yet
huka puétata téa #
that gate   find

1. And now, though having shut the gate himself, he cannot find it, 2. and is walking along the fence, partly holding himself up on the little sharp points of the fence boards. 3. And now he's standing straight at the corner where he piled the wood, 4. but still he hasn't found the gate yet.

29

1. ʔika yoémta háibu símsuk íntok huʔu koní óri + ʔim káata bépa + ʔín wáam + néʔeka #
   this man already gone and the raven the there house over here by flew
2. ʔiʔi yoém íntok + humak + hunuka káa tuʔúreka # ʔómot bičá yéu síika #
   this man and might that not liking else-where toward out went

1. After the man had gone a raven flew over the house. 2. It might be this man, not liking this, went out elsewhere.

30

1. ramáa čeaʔ + koní tosáta + béna + 2. hitáʔekun + huʔu koní + humak áman + bemélasi
   ramada more raven nest like that's-why the raven maybe there new
tosátebáeka # 3. ʔáe bépa hikát iʔan kátek #
nest-wants on-it on-top up now sitting

1. The ramada looks much like a raven's nest. 2. That's why the raven wants to make a new nest 3. and is sitting up on top of it.

31

1. huʔu ramáa wóikatána káá sáptitáka + huʔu koní bépa kátekasú + néʔeka # ʔáetuk + yéu
   the ramada other-side not walled the raven over sitting-after flew under out
síika 2. bóetuk huʔu sápti kaíta hum bináa botana ínto wánaa botana huniʔi + hunéʔela #
went because the wall nothing there this side and other side even bare

1. The ramada, not being walled, the raven who was sitting on top flew under it and went out, 2. since there is no wall on this side and it is bare on the other side.

32

1. kia hunúen (am) ama náh nénnéʔek íntum + kári behúʔukú + káteka + 2. hukáʔa sámíta
   just thus there about flying and-there house eaves-at sitting that adobe
+ tosá yáʔabáemta benási ʔam ʔááne tá kááma ʔáwe # húmakúʔu #
nest make-wanting like it doing but not-there able might

1. Just flying around thus, he sits under the eaves 2. acting as though he wants to make a nest on the adobe. But he might not be able to do it.

33

1. twísi báisi huʔu + kárita bépa # náh kóósuka íntok + ʔían ínto huʔu kárita bépa + káteka hum
   good thrice the house over about lying and now and the house on sitting there
ramáu bičá púhhúbaka # 2. káteka ʔamán + ʔaʔa bítčú + humák + ket húmak áman +
ramada toward facing sitting yonder it looking maybe yet maybe yonder
tosátebáe #
nest-wants

1. After having flown thrice over the house he is now sitting facing the ramada. 2. He (is) looking yonder. He might even want to build a nest there.

34

1. čéʔawasu kía huka yoémta ama ʔánsuka benásia + ʔiní wíkit kia bemélas humak kía +
   and-even-worse yet that man there done-have like this bird just anew maybe just

2. nóólia   náh   wéltatáitek   + 3. kóram met yéhték + ʔínto ramáa   met yéhték into huʔu
   repeatedly about circling-started   fences on sitting   and   ramada on sitting and the
kári bépa + yéhsúka   iʔan 3. into húči korát bépa kátek áman + tebáčiu kóom bítčú #
house over having-sat now and again fence on sits yonder   yard-to down looking

1. And now the worst is that this bird is acting like the man has been doing. 2. He has started circling about the house all over anew. And he is sitting on top of the fences, and on top of the ramada, and after sitting on top of the house 3. again (he is) sitting on the fence and looking down toward the yard.

35

1. huʔu kóra betána (hikáu) + hikáu néʔeka húʔu + kári bépa + séhtuli yéhtéka + 2. ʔíntuči   #
   the fence from   up   flew   the   house over   once sitting   and-again
hikáu béenóʔoteka   + ʔíntuči   ramáata bépa + (húnen) húnen + sáikulímakasú   #
up   flew-to-and-from   and-again ramada over   thus   circling-having-been
3. béa   íʔantúči   káata bépa káteka + 4. húči hum ramáu bičá   bitčú + huʔu wíikit #
   already now-and-again house over sitting   again there ramada toward looking   the bird

1. Flying from the fence he sat down once on top of the house 2. and again he flew back and forth over the ramada, thus having been circling. 3. Now again he is sitting on top of the house. 4. The bird is looking toward the ramada.

36

1. béntanapo áman   hum káriu   kíbakeka íntok humá   # ʔáma wáiwa áu   páttáika áu
   window-on through there house-to entered and   maybe there inside himself closed   himself
téaka humá ʔoʔómteka 2. káain   ʔánmáčika wosábáisi + ʔama wéltaka # húči húm # 3. sékáʔana
found maybe angry   not-how do-could twice-thrice there circling again there   other
béntanapo táʔata yéu wée betána húči kúkti   áma yéu néʔeka + 4. ʔian ínto háu   bičá
window-on sun   out went from again sound-of-wings there out flying   now and where toward
humá símla káábe ʔim mačísia #
maybe gone nobody here visible

1. Going on through the window he entered the house. Maybe there inside he found himself closed in and maybe got angry. 2. Not knowing what to do he circled twice or thrice and again. 3. Then going through the window that is toward the sunrise, he is coming out with a loud sound of wings. 4. And now perhaps he is gone for no one can be seen around here.

37

1. níí wíkit huma tečóe   háʔani + 2. má čéa   + huʔu kúhta bépa + kátek # 3. ʔii ʔínto
   this bird might do-bad-omen somehow   so   more   the cross upon   sitting   this and
yoéme háksuma yéu síka háibu húči áman ʔáanéka hum kúhta bépa aʔa kátek # ʔáu yépsáka
man   there-from out came already again yonder being   there cross on it sitting   to-it arrived
mékka áʔa bébak   #
away it   chased (whipped)

1. This bird might be of bad omen somehow. 2. The worst is that it is now sitting on top of the cross 3. and this man, coming out from somewhere again, is again there by the cross. He arrived and whipped away the bird.

38

1. katíʔín ne sépnóóka + (ʔaʔa) ʔaa tečóe   tía ikáʔa koníta bóetuk huka yoémta hunuén +
   not-did I at-once-say   it of-bad-omen say this raven because this man   that-way

mékka á?a bébak # húči hum + pá?aka ?a wé?ek # 2. ?áe bépa + háreki wewéltakasu +
far it chase again there outside it standing him over repeatedly circled-having
?íntúči # ?á?a tóó síka 3. ?ián íntuči káabe húmak + hakún bičá síika #
and-again it left went now and-again no-one maybe where toward gone

1. Didn't I say at once that it is of bad omen, this raven, because the man chased it away when he was standing outside. 2. Having repeatedly circled over him now again it left him and now again it is not there. 3. I don't know where it is gone.

39

1. ?íntuči huka yoémta símsuk íntuči hakú?ubo sumá yeú siká # ?íntuči + kó?om +
  and-again that man gone-being and-again somewhere maybe out came and-again down
yepsáka hum ramáata bétúk # 2. híta + tečí?ikemta benási ?áma ?áane + hum + túa
arrived the ramada under what scratches-on-ground-who like there doing there truly
kútata wé?eka náápo #
wood stand near

1. And when the man was gone again, it (the bird) again came from somewhere, and came down under the ramada. 2. It was doing as though it was scratching on the ground near the post.

40

1. ?ían hú?u wíkit híbu túa amá tosátebáe # 2. má čé?a húka + ?a?a tosátené + ?a?a
  now the bird perhaps truly there nest-wants so more that it nest-will it
totóhitáitek 3. tá káá im ramáata bépa tosátebáe # 4. má čéa ?omót bičá huka huyáta
carry-started but not here ramada upon nest-want so more elsewhere toward the brush
wéiya #
carrying

1. Now the bird perhaps truly wants to make a nest there, 2. so that it started to carry the brush it wants to make the nest with. 3. It seems that it doesn't want to build the nest upon the ramada, 4. so is carrying the brush elsewhere.

41

1. hu?ubwan sé?eboim káábem áané?epo huni + wepúlaika hu?u sé?ebói ?im yépsáka túa
  that-being houseflies not-one existing-where even a-single the fly here came truly
hum + sámí kárit hikáu + weámaka # ?íntuči kóom bičá + ?áet weáma #
there adobe house-on up walking and-again down toward on-it walk

1. There being no flies here, one fly came and is actually walking up and down the adobe house.

42

1. ?ían ínti?i sámít hikáu + táhtáhti weámsuka 2. huka yoémta hum pá?aku
  now and-this adobe-on up through walked-having that man there outside
weámamta téaka + 3. ?áman béewata áu áaneka + 4. hu?u yoém ínto + ?a?a čóontaitek háisa
is-walking-who finding yonder teasing him doing the man and it slapping how
a?a símtuaka 5. háusa bíča huma síika #
it gone-made where toward might go

1. And now after having walked up and down on the adobe 2. it finds the man who is walking outside.

3. It goes yonder and acts as though it is teasing him. 4. The man started slapping at it and made it go away 5. (and now I don't know) where he might have gone.

43

1. ʔiníisan séʔebói inímika yoémta káá ʔama ʔéltúameʔ # tábanót titéuwáwáu #. 2. bóetu iní
   this-is fly   this   man not there ease horsefly is-called   because these
kabáʔim + ʔáanéʔepo híba ket # tábano áma weámne # 3. ʔiní má óʔóu ʔian + kábáita áma
horses   exist-where always truly   horsefly there walk-will   this so man now   horse there
yéu tóhak   hum kórapo + ʔíntok # áet haháʔamu + 4. tá íntok + ket huni únna wákíla má
out brought there fence-in and   on-it mounting   but and   yet even very skinny so
čéʔa + (káá) + káá ʔa túa yúumaka   yoémeta humak áuwi háʔani huʔu yoéme #
more   not   him truly unable-to-carry man   maybe fat-is perhaps the man

1. This fly that is keeping the man from being at ease is called the horsefly, 2. because where there are horses the horsefly is always seen around. 2. This man now brought the horse inside the fence and is attempting to mount it, 4. but it (the horse) is very skinny and the man is perhaps very fat so the horse is unable to carry him.

44

1. ʔiʔi yoéme hum kórapo huka kábáita yéu tóhaka # ʔápeláik + ʔámaʔ + tóó siká # kía húkaʔa
   this man there fence-at that horse out brought   alone   there left went just that
báhta áma áʔa montóriak 2. huʔu kábáʔi into kía seséstul + ʔáu nóinóiteka
grass there it piled   the horse and just once-in-a-while to-it goes-back-and-forth
ilí amá áʔa bwáʔe #
little there it eating

1. This man, having brought the horse inside the fence, made a pile of hay and left it (the horse) alone. 2. The horse every once in a while goes to the grass eating a little of it.

45

1. ʔían ínto húka kábáʔita + hákun   omót   tóhaka + ʔíntok čúʔú íntiʔan áu
   now and that horse   somewhere elsewhere taking   and   dog and-now to-him
yépsák # ʔáma yéusisime # ʔían 2. íntok áma + kúh náapo   ʔa bóʔotek # íntáu
came   there playing   now   and   there cross near-where it laying   and-to-him
bóʔoka + ʔáʔa bítču + ʔilí čúʔú #
laid   him looking little dog

1. Now the man took the horse somewhere else and the dog came to him and now it is playing with him. 2. Now when he laid down near the cross the little dog laid down beside him and is looking at him.

46

1. huʔu wíkit hum + (kóra −) kórapo weámaʔakasú # 2. ʔían húka + káró hekkáta bitčáka into
   the bird there   fence-on walked-having now that   car shade   seeing and
túa karóta betúk + yéhték ama káá yéu síika #
truly car under   car   under not out came

1. The bird, having walked on the fence, 2. saw the shade of the car and went under the car and didn't come out.

47

1. ʔían íntok huma húka hékkáta káá túʔúreka + hukaʔa # tomóbilta (káabeta áma + ʔáanemta bi-)
   now and maybe that shade not liking that automobile
káabeta áma áanémta bitčáka # ʔáe bépa hikat háʔamuka # ʔáe bepa hikát kátek #
nobody there being seeing on-it top up climbed on-it top up sitting

1. And now maybe he doesn't like that shade. 2. Seeing no one around the automobile he climbed up, sitting on top of it.

48

1. kía hábetaka hunumak + makínata bitčáʔatek ʔaa túʔúlene # 2. ʔyan má húʔu wíkit + mékka
   just anybody even-might motor seeing-if it like-would now so the bird far
bičá néʔekasu íntuči nóttek + kía áetuk yéu húʔubúteka # 3. húči hikáu čátka #
away flew and-again returned yet under out flying again up hovering

1. Anyone would probably just love the motor if they saw it. 2. So now the bird, after flying far away, returned again and is just getting under it, 3. and then again hovering in the air.

CONVERSATION TEXT

Note: an asterisk indicates the person who is not carrying the conversational ball at the moment has just said ʔmmMm, meaning about the same thing as *heewi* in Yaqui, or un-huh in English. These vocal nods usually occur near the end of a span, but sometimes anticipate the end and begin in the middle of a span final word. Dots indicate intentional omission of phrases or names. The following is only a part of the recorded conversation.

R-1

1. nák katíʔin itón usímsuk + ná ʔánia + ʔitóm + ʔáet rehtísuka + ket húni tuísi hiápsan
   then isn't-it-so we children-were that world we on-it wandered yet even very lively
bóetuk báʔá húʔebenáekan intok ité intok # 2. ʔáet kia híba pásealó restémča
because water much-was and we moreover on-it just always joy-wandering traveling-as
réhtem # 3. káá húnen //
traveled not that way?

1. When we were children the world was still very lively, isn't it so? And the places we used to wander because much water was there! 2. and we traveled about it just as though always joy-wandering ("spreading about the country like a flood"). 3. Is it not that way?

F-1

1. ʔéew katíín te # béa ória # sílba lékipó im + ʔóri + ... sílba léki bóʔót sahák
   yes didn't we already ah! silver lake-at there ah silver lake road-on went
béa + áhta hum représom meu yaháka # * kattíín te béa * ʔáma ʔúʔbane # * 2. ʔáma
already up-to there dam to arriving didn't we already there swam-would there
ʔúʔbásuk * bea té # * amák te húči nóttine # * ʔámak + ʔíntim + káwi
swam-after already we sometimes we again return-will sometime and-here mountain
áákamtta + bétukún bičá + * matánsaú bičá sakáʔane # *
that-has-pitaya under toward slaughter-house-to toward go-would

CONVERSATION TEXT

1. Yes, didn't we? There at Silver Lake, on Silver Lake Road, we went up to the dam, and isn't it so, we used to swim there. 2. And after swimming we used to come back here sometimes and sometimes we would go toward the mountain which has pitaya on it to the slaughter house.

R-2

1. né ket áu wáasuk bóetuk té + hunáet náu ré?erehtísuk # ?íbo tana óri + misyón
I yet it remember because we that-part together wandered-have this side ah! mission
bóót túa tána íntok + ...ta   matánsapo
road-on truly from more   (name 1 of owner of the slaughter house) slaughter-house-at
húči # 2. ?ínto + sáuwom   bwáseo ínto sáuwom méu bíča sáhaka ínto hunámen ínto
again and saguaro-apples ripening and saguaros to toward going and yonder and
híapne   #
spearing-down

1. I still remember it because we wandered that part together, from this side, on the mission road, to _____'s slaughter house again. 2. And when the saguaro fruit was ripening we used to go toward the saguaro forest. And there we would spear down the fruit with a long stick (híapne).

F-2

1. ?eéwi // ?óousi te katíín áet rehtisuk hunáeči hunáek ínto te béa híapsuk +
yes manly we didn't on-it wandered then-again then and we already speared-down
béha # 2. húči am núk nóttine hunak béa te # ?íntuči húm représompo ú?úbak
already again them carrying returned then already we and-again there dam-at swam
béa katíín te béha # * 3. ?áhta + ?ú?ubásuk bea húči saká?áne sáuwom * béha *
already isn't-it-so we already up-to swam-have already again go-would saguaro already
wéíyeak # * ?áhta * itóm hóawi + * ?ám tóhine   #
carry up-to our home-to them deliver-would

1. Yes. We used to wander manfully about, and after having picked the saguaro fruit 2. then we would carry them, and again swim there at the dam, isn't it so? 3. After having swam then we went away carrying the saguaro fruit to our home, and delivered them.

R-3

1. nák né + ket húni unna ilíčiakan bóetuk ketúni + ne báát únná mékka kó?omi ku
then I yet even very little-was because yet-even I water very far down where
ketúni + 2. káá ?áman kíbakeka bea emé ne téhwálatune maiyóau + né + ?íno
yet-even not yonder entering already you(pl.) me informed edge-of-lake-to I myself
uhú?u sáekai # 3. ?ínto + ánima ...tukau huná ínto sákwéeka bea né aman
nursing told and the-deceased (name 2) who-was he and sometimes already me yonder
núk kíbakebae ?eme náwit + komímpo ne tobó?o namáka ne hum mékka kó?omi kú
with enter-want you (pl.) both arms-by me lift carrying-along me there far deep where
ne bahúmtúa # ?émpo ?aú wáate   //
me swim-cause-to you(sg.) of-it remember?

1. In those days I was still very young because I could not go into the deep water. 2. Not being able to go into the deep water, you had informed me to stay at the edge of the lake. 3. And (name 2), who is now deceased, sometimes decided to take me yonder, so you both carry me by the arms, pick me up and carry me along into the deep water and force me to swim. You remember it?

F-3

1. ʔéewi // né au wáate katíʔín // * 2. hunáksan té énči + báhúm mahtáʔamaʔa #
   yes   I of-it remember isn't-it-so   by-that-time we you(sg.) swim teaching
(F *laughs*) ....
1. Yes, I remember, isn't it so? By that time we were teaching you to swim.

R-4

1. héeu +
   yes
1. Yes.

F-4

1. héewi #
   yes
1. Yes.

R-5

... 1. animáʔuri ...   tukau   ilí pappáu * katíʔín híba intómak wéwéʔaman # .... 2.
      the-deceased (name 3) who-was little Papago isn't-it-so always us-with wander
hunáemak   té béha   ínim + máiyóat   híba úʔubátuan   3. áhta ké béa   + té +
that-one-with we already here edge-of-lake always swimming-made up-to not already we
ʔinto báhúm máhtáka beha   hum mékka koʔomi kún   kíkímu háptek # 4. kááʔ into hinélwači
and   swim learning already there far down where entered started   not more no-danger
teúpo #
saying
1. Wasn't it so that the deceased (name 3) the little Papago boy, always used to wander with us all the time? 2. With him I used to be swimming always at the edge of the lake, 3. until we learned to swim, and then we started going into the deep water, 4. like saying, there's no more danger now.

F-5

1. ʔéeu sííme ku # hunée ne wáate   * ... háibu # * 2. ne ilí + * yóʔówe # * 3. hun tuan
   yes all that those I remember already   I little   grown-up   so then
té itépo   béha + * ʔénčim uhúʔúsasákan #
we ourselves already   you(pl.) nursing
1. Yes, I remember all that. 2. I was already a little grownup. 3. So that's why we were still nursing you.

R-6

1. héewi +
   yes
1. Yes.

F-6

1. ʔénčim ilíčiaku # * ʔíntok wáʔák sénu katíín   óri # ʔóri ...
   you(pl.) little-were   and that one isn't-it-so ah ah (name 4)
1. You were still very young. And the other one, isn't it so, (name 4) ---

R-7

1. héewi
   yes
1. Yes.

F-7

1. ...
   (name 4)
1. (name 4) ---

R-8

1. hunáa   túa   itómak wéweaman #
   that-one truly us-with wandered
1. That one wandered about with us very much

F-8

1. héewi huná?a itómak weáma # hákuuní?í háibu itómak áu   kwéntane katí?íne #
   yes   that-one us-with wander where-even already us-with himself accounted isn't-it-so
1. Yes, that one wandered with us. Wherever he was, he was always ready to count himself with us, isn't it so?

R-9

1. ?éewa   into + ?áu   ómteka + ?itóm aa kónkóntaria itómak yéu ?a síiko # 2. hulén su
   mother-his and   to-him angry   us   him intercepted us-with out him went   thus then
   béha   amak   káá itómak símne   íntok #
   already sometimes not us-with go-would and
1. And his mother used to intercept him as he tried to sneak off and go away with us. 2. Thus sometimes he wasn't able to go with us.

F-9

1. ?itómak étbwa bwítine   #
   us-with steal run-would
1. And sometimes he used to sneak out with us.

R-10

1. héewi húnen áanen   //
   yes   thus do-would
1. Yes, that's what he used to do.

F-10

1. ?áanen #
   do-would
1. He'd do (that).

R-11

1. ʔinén into hiúsimne   te áman yahákatek čúbatuk   te kía kamóten   benásia hum
   thus and saying-would we yonder arrived-if after-a-little-while we just sweet-potatoes like   there
báʔápo čáʔásasakane #
water-on floating-will

(*Both laugh, then several seconds of silence follow.*)

1. And when he was coming with us he used to say thus, "If you get there, in a little while you will be floating like sweet potatoes!"

F-11

1. ʔiʔánsu béa   hakún bičáʔ // kéé   čupéʔ //
   now-then already where toward   not-yet finished?
1. Now then where to? Isn't it finished yet?

R-12

1. híba   wéye // híba   wéye //
   always goes   always goes
1. It's still going! It's still going!

F-12

1. héeu pós hunuéni bwan usímtaka   ʔaa úhyóilíne huka báʔáta 2. katíʔíne béha + kía
   yes well thus   so   children-being it enjoy   that water   isn't-it-so? already just
híba +
always

1. Yes, when we were children we used to love the water very much, 2. isn't it so? Always ___ __

R-13

1. ʔúsira   hunéʔela #
   childhood carefree
1. Childhood is carefree.

F-13

1. ʔúsira   + béha   + hunéʔela # ʔúhyóilímta * benási + úʔúbakái + * hiápsi hotéʔenemta *
   childhood   already   carefree   enjoying   like   swimming   heart settle-down
benási túa tatáek huni katíʔín te kía háisa úʔúbane   # *
like   truly warm even isn't-it-so we just how   swim-would

1. Thus is childhood. We seem to have been enjoying everything and we felt the heart would settle down, even when it was hot, by going into the water and swimming, isn't it so?

R-14

1. kía hiókot   ʔéewame kía káá bétte túa   bečíʔibo íntok huʔu pótéʔot
   just suffering feeling   just not heavy truly for   and that fenced-property-used-for-cattle
pásealó   # 2. híba báʔá púsipo íntok huʔu ʔóri + ...   ta matánsa betána # 3. hunáman
joy-wandering   always water spring and the ah   (name 5)   slaughter from   up-yonder

into bákeom into bákeom íntitón gómgómtane itóm čóčóʔilabáekai # 4. ʔénči su (*laughs*) túa
and cowboys and cowboys and-us scaring us lassoing-wanting you(sg.) next truly
buési wéiyeáne huʔu + ... katíine # * ....
largely carrying that (name 5) isn't-it-so?

1. Even if we were striving so much we did not have a heavy feeling, and the places on the cattle field, 2. and over on the water spring, and over on this side toward (name 5)'s slaughter house! 3. And the cowboys up yonder used to frighten us and try to lasso us. 4. That (name 5) used to carry you most of the time isn't it so?

F-14

1. bué itón usíle ínto káá áma itón + hítása + bénak itón * hóʔiʔa + 2. hum háksa * kútam
   well us children and not there us whatever like us do   there what wood
káá itóm áma yéu wikíáane * katíine # 3. hunén béha + * húka potéota súáka ama
not us there out take-would isn't-it-so? thus already that cattle-field watching there
weámne # * káá báʔekai #
wandered   not wanting

1. Seeing that we were children he hated to see us do anything on his property. 2. He didn't want us to take any wood off the property, 3. thus he used to guard the cattle field.

R-15

1. séstul waʔa ... bákeo katíʔín áma hiba yóo bákeo hum matánsapo huná
   once that (name 6) cowboy isn't-it-so there always elder cowboy there slaughter-house-at that-one
óri + ket + itóm hum + sámí kári kónila háhásekasu # kabái into áet wéček ínto máča
ah yet us there adobe house around chasing-then horse and on-it fell and leg
síotak háisa ʔa yáak + 2. kasóke béngwa lóitukan # 3. hunuén émo ʔíʔabáekái
sprained how him made case-is long-time limping thus themselves being-grouchy-desiring
bea hunúka ama bítčák # kia úsim + kábáimak #
already that there saw just children horse-with

1. And once the cowboy, (name 6), isn't it so?, a longtime cowboy at the slaughterhouse, used to chase us around the house on horseback, and doing so the horse fell on him and sprained a leg. 2. The case is he was limping. 3. Just because they wanted to be cross with the children this is what happened to them.